MW00605544

HOODOO FOR BEGINNERS

WORKING MAGIC SPELLS IN ROOTWORK AND CONJURE WITH ROOTS, HERBS, CANDLES, AND OILS

ANGELIE BELARD

HENTOPAN
PUBLISHING

CONTENTS

SPECIAL OFFER FROM HENTOPAN PUBLISHING

Get this additional book by Angela Belard just for signing up.

Hundreds of others are already enjoying insider access to all of our current and future books, 100% free!

If you want insider access, plus this free book, scan the QR code below with your phone!

INTRODUCTION

I had just turned 23 when Mama Estelle was buried. She was my favorite person in this world. Mama Estelle was my grandmother, but everyone loved her. I know that we all say this about our grandmothers, but this is the honest truth about Mama Estelle. She was exceptional. She raised me, for the most part, even though I did spend some time with my parents. Most of who I am as a woman today can be attributed to Mama Estelle. This book begins on the day she was buried because that was the day the rest of my life began. Throughout my life, right up to the moment she died, Mama Estelle would sit me down and tell me stories about her childhood and share secrets with me about our way of life.

Hoodoo for her was not some folklore or black magic, although certain aspects of it could take on a really dark tone. Still, it wasn't this dark and mysterious thing that has been portrayed in the movies. It was about being attuned to your environment and knowing your roots, understanding the power of your ancestors and manipulating the elements in your favor. Unfortunately, I never really appreciated any of this until the day I saw Mama Estelle being put into the earth. And so, there I sat, listening to the slow, monotonous sound of the priest reciting the final rites. Mama Estelle was a devout member of the small local church and many people knew and loved her. I was physically present to witness the somber event taking place around me, but I felt as though I was somewhere else.

What registered the most in my mind was the thick air of silence that seemed to envelope the whole graveyard. When it was time to pick up dirt and pour it on the coffin, I thought I wouldn't be able to do it. I thought it would break me for sure. But the moment my hands connected with earth, I experienced what felt like a transference of energy. I felt peace and quiet so intense that it felt as though I was betraying the grief I was feeling inside. You could say the day Mama Estelle was buried was the day I was reborn. Because right there by her grave site was where I became consciously aware of the powers that surround us. Of the divinity that dwells on the inside of us. It was that day all of her teachings came alive for me.

It has been over 40 years since that moment when I made the decision to become a Hoodoo practitioner, and I have never looked back. Now, I want to honor Mama Estelle's legacy by sharing some of her wealth of knowledge, in addition to some of my own experiences in the practice of Hoodoo.

I don't know what brought you to this book. Most of my clients come to see me when something in their life has gone very wrong, and they've already tried all the "normal" ways to fix it. Some come out of plain old curiosity. Maybe you're just looking for a simple spell to make your life a little easier to bear. Whatever it is that brought you here, you should know that there are no coincidences in this life. I hope my book can help you find what you're looking for, and maybe find something even more important than that.

This book is foundational knowledge of the practice of Hoodoo. If you are looking for academic research, you won't find much here, because everything I know, and everything I have done, has been passed down from mother to daughter for generations. Some of the information is unique to my family. But it will serve you well just as it has served my family and clients and all those we have helped. In this book you will find:

- A brief history on Hoodoo and some common misconceptions
- A foundational knowledge of key elements of Hoodoo practices
- A breakdown of the symbolism of purification rites and their application in day-to-day life
- How to create an enabling environment for spells to manifest
- Simple and powerful spells for love, luck, money and life in general

Before you delve into Chapter 1, I urge you to proceed with an open mind. At the end of the day, your mind is the birthplace of whatever spell or enchantment you will cast. If you are filled with doubt, unresolved emotions and negative thoughts in general, especially about the practice itself, you may find that most of what you learn will be rendered impotent.

So be open-minded, be generous with your positive emotions and most importantly, embrace the power that is within you.

1

MY HOODOO ROOTS

The first Hoodoo working I performed without help from Mama Estelle was for a young man who was just setting up a convenience store. This was his third attempt at starting a business, and after previous failures, he was worried that he was cursed. For a novice, this was a lot of pressure on me. I could barely put a protection spell together and here I was being called on to reverse the misfortunes of this man and invite wealth into his life.

I started with a floor wash of his store, using roots and herbs that cleanse and protect, and a few more to draw luck and money. After cleansing the floor, I cleansed the door and the path leading to the store. When we finished with the cleanse, I buried nine pennies at the entrance, underneath earth that had been dug up from a bank, along with a lodestone, and then sealed this by pouring quality whiskey over it. Two weeks later, the store opened. Six months after that, he opened another branch in another part of town and then just kept growing. In the decades following my first attempt, I have performed this cleanse and money attraction spell several times, and each time it has been effective.

I imagine that you are currently just starting out your journey as a Hoodoo practitioner and you want to find effective ways to achieve results. You have probably taken note of this money invitation spell and perhaps even put down the book long enough to put the ingredients together. The spell I mentioned above is one of the basic beginner spells. At the end of this book, I am certain that you will be able to create your own money spell, change your fortune in the process and do a whole lot more. But I am also sure that there is a logical side of you that is seeking an explanation as to how the elements I listed above; the coins, the lodestone and the earth from the bank, were able to manifest wealth.

To see the connection between all these things and the world that lies beyond our physical realm, you need to peer behind the curtain and expand the borders of your mind. Now, because it was easy for me to accept my transition into Hoodoo practice, I know that I will not completely understand what you are struggling with. That said, I should point out that I firmly believe my first ritual was effective for one primary reason - I believed it would work. If this is completely new to you, this is going to be a journey that will require you to change your perspective about certain things.

So, why was it easy for me to believe? I was the love child of a young Haitian immigrant and a Creole girl. They were too young to raise a child, so I ended up with my grandmother. My mother later married another man. I spent some time at both my mother's house and my father's, but most of my childhood was spent with Mama Estelle. I suppose my childhood was a bit odd, but it helped me see things differently from the way others saw them.

In the Beginning...

Growing up with Mama Estelle, Hoodoo was always a part of my life. I never had to go through training or any kind of ceremony to be introduced to it. I saw it around the house just the way you probably saw things in your childhood. Like the herbs in your mother's kitchen or the newspaper that was always lying on the coffee table, or the toys in your playroom. It was natural to me in my day-to-day life.

For example, when my grandmother had a headache, she would never take aspirin. Instead she would make a tincture from specific herbs and spices. She would take this mixture and go to sleep, and when she woke up she would be right as rain. And she always had a white cloth with a candle on it beside her bed. I didn't think anything of what I suspect would seem bizarre to you. It wasn't until Mama Estelle explained it that I realized it was part of a protection spell.

Growing Up With a Hoodoo Background

Mama Estelle descended from a long line of Hoodoo practitioners who go back generations, and for her this was a way of life. She never shied away from her identity and was very proud to be recognized as a "two-headed" doctor. It wasn't just a title for her. People came to her for solutions. I remember a woman who traveled across the country to come and see Mama Estelle. She was desperate to get pregnant and had been trying for several years. Medicine hadn't made the advancements that it has today, and even the little that was available in the way of fertility treatment was too expensive. So, in her desperation, she sought out my grandmother.

That night, my grandmother performed the fertility ritual. She asked me to witness it because I was a young woman and she explained that my energy would help make the ritual more effective. It was a beautiful ceremony and in my young eyes it was both magical and mysterious. The woman and her husband had moved into town so that they could be closer to my grandmother in order to be able to receive her regular herbal treatment. I didn't think anything of this until six months later we ran into her at the store. She was pregnant and glowing. I cannot count the number of times I witnessed miracles such as these. It was just a part of growing up and I think this is one of the reasons I took it for granted, that is, until I lost my grandmother.

Sharing My Rich but Mysterious Heritage

People have many misconceptions about Hoodoo, and in this book I want to try as much as possible to address most, if not all of them. I want to start by letting you know that Hoodoo is not some mysterious dark force that taints your life. In truth, it can enhance your experiences and help you navigate very difficult moments.

Hoodoo is as spiritual as it is physical. There are aspects of Hoodoo practice that simply focus on the use of herbs. The idea generally is to connect with nature. Mother Earth is the most powerful element in the world. She is home to the soil that is a direct link to our ancestors. She is the conduit for light and life, and if you channel her essence, you can bring about productivity and multiplication in your life. Practicing Hoodoo gives you a very pragmatic perspective about life. For instance, your views about certain objects or places are no longer tainted by negative emotions like fear, anger or pain. Instead, you are able to see these places as connections to a world beyond our physical world. I know that sounds mysterious so I will give you an example. The cemetery is generally regarded as sacred ground where our loved ones are put to rest. But there have been a lot of dark notions perpetuated about the cemetery as a place or gathering of evil. This is far from the truth. A graveyard is a source of immense power. This power can be channeled for good or for evil. It is as simple as that.

In the next chapter, I will talk about the history of Hoodoo, and hopefully bring you to a place of understanding. With better understanding, you open yourself up to the benefits of Hoodoo practice.

2

THE HISTORY OF HOODOO

Hoodoo, Conjure, or Rootwork, as it is sometimes called, can be traced back to the arrival of enslaved Africans here in America. When our ancestors arrived here, the African practices that they came with merged with European and Native American influences. African beliefs and customs met with European folklore and the botanical knowledge of American Indians came together under one umbrella - Hoodoo.

People consulted with Hoodoo doctors when they needed spiritual help. Whether it had to do with physical health or changing their fortunes for the better, Hoodoo was always used to make the lives of people easier and better. Slave owners, however, tried to vilify African spiritual practices, calling it demonic or devil worship or witchcraft. If you've ever heard negative things about Hoodoo, that's where it all started.

A Spiritual Journey

In my personal opinion (and I believe this is a sentiment shared by many who practice Hoodoo), Hoodoo is more of a personalized spiritual journey than it is anything else. In a religion, you worship a deity, something considered supernatural and supreme. This deity, or in some cases, multiple deities, dictates what is right or wrong, good or evil. In Hoodoo, however, you are free to practice any religion, or none at all, and still practice Hoodoo.

In Hoodoo, you create your own personal magic using the knowledge you have of the various roots, herbs and other elements. It is about establishing a connection with the spirits around us. It is a way of life. There is no devotion that you have to perform, other than the physical rituals required for the results that you demand.

In the practice of Hoodoo, magic comes from roots, stones, bones and even discharge from the human body, such as blood, sweat and so on. By combining their power, you are able to tap into the force it produces and channel it to deliver the results you want. Your desired results could range from healing to jinxing, love potions to money spells and much more. You have the ability to manifest whatever it is you desire. All you need is knowledge of the right combination of these elements and acceptance of the power that you possess. But most importantly, you need to acknowledge and have a reverence for the spirits of our ancestors. In Hoodoo, we understand that there are spirits constantly around us, and those spirits can either serve or harm, depending on how you treat them. I will get into more of that later but for now, just understand that Hoodoo has less to do with faith and more to do with changing fate.

Voodoo vs. Hoodoo

A lot of people use Voodoo and Hoodoo interchangeably, thinking that they mean the same thing, but you need to understand that while they have roots in central African religions, they are very different practices. Think of them as distant cousins, at best.

Voodoo is a religion primarily practiced in Haiti. There is a similar, but distinct practice also called Voodoo in Louisiana. Practitioners of both forms of Voodoo serve the Lwa, powerful spirits believed to control the physical world. Haitian Voodoo is more a religion than Louisiana Voodoo, with regular congregations and initiated priests. Louisiana Voodoo is less of what you might think of as a religion, but beyond that, there's not much of a distinction between the two. You'll meet people who practice Voodoo in all kinds of ways.

Hoodoo is not a religion at all, and worship and service to the Lwa is not part of it. That's probably the best way to draw a line between Hoodoo and Voodoo - if the Lwa are involved, it's definitely Voodoo.

Hoodoo and Christianity

When African slaves were brought to North America, they were not allowed to practice their old religions. Slaves were forcibly baptized into Christianity, either Catholicism or Protestantism, depending on their owners. They had to hide their old religious practices under a veil of Christianity.

Many aspects of Christianity weren't so very different from traditional African religions. The African slaves already believed in one creator, God. Many believed in powerful spirits that helped run the world, and recognized Catholic Saints as just another aspect of those spirits. The Bible was seen as a powerful spell book, and even today many traditional Hoodoo workings include reading various psalms while casting a spell.

Mama Estelle was a devout Baptist and took me to church with her every Sunday. After the service was over, I would see people go up to her and talk quietly. Sometimes she would hand them small objects, and sometimes I saw them hand her money. For Mama Estelle, and the people she helped, there was no conflict between their Christianity and their belief in the power of Hoodoo.

Hopefully, I have been able to open your mind concerning some of the most difficult areas of understanding Hoodoo. The next step is to delve deeper into the practice and our first stop will be to look at those elements that I have been talking about. In the next chapter, I will focus on seven important elements of Hoodoo. As you continue your study and practice of Hoodoo outside of this book, you will learn a lot more on this subject. But for now, these seven elements are your starting point.

3

THE ELEMENTS OF HOODOO

In many magical practices, the elements focused on evolve around water, air, fire and earth. In Hoodoo practice, the force in these elements is recognized but the practice goes a lot deeper. We see the connection between the things in the world around us and the spiritual realm. There is also a lot of symbolism and representative magic used to create spells that are potent and life-altering. In this chapter, I will highlight some fundamental forces that power Hoodoo practice and explain how spirits interact with these elements. Your understanding of this concept will be very useful in helping you create and develop your very own personalized Mojo, spell or ritual. You should understand that the more unique a spell is to you, the greater the chances of it working for you.

The spells that I will share with you in this book are standard spells that are very effective. However, every situation is different, and if you can craft your own spell specific to your own needs, the results will be far more powerful.

Your understanding of individual roots and the power they hold is a crucial factor in determining the potency of a spell. Think of it like going to the grocery store to buy some vegetables because you want to get healthy. Vegetables are good for you in general, but if you know what each vegetable is best for with regard to your health goals, you can buy the right ones for you. Likewise, choosing the roots that are right for your particular magical needs will save you time, money, and will help you achieve better results.

I had a client who used to have a problem that perfectly illustrates the message I am trying to get across. She was in love with a man and they had been in a relationship for a long time, but suddenly he started drifting away from her. Now, she knew that he loved her, but he was having difficulty staying focused on that love and their relationship. So, she went online and found some love potions. For the first few days after administering the love potion, everything seemed to be going well. But within a few weeks, they would be back to struggling with the same problems again. This went on for several months until she came to see me. She assumed that she had not performed the ritual and the spell well enough or that perhaps it was completely wrong. But this was not the problem.

The problem was that she was using a general love drawing spell - but the man already loved her. She needed something unique to her situation. Oftentimes I'll prescribe a series of steps for a client to take to bring about the result they're looking for, and in this case we began with a love drawing bath that included coriander, because it brings about fidelity. We followed this with a candle spell using a red candle and cinnamon to add some heat to the relationship. It worked well for my client. They've been married for over a decade now.

Ancestral Spirits

We are often called to "know" ourselves. We translate this to mean knowing our likes, our dislikes, our socio-cultural identity and connecting with our innermost thoughts. All of this is fantastic because having a strong sense of self is necessary for making your way in this world today. How else will you be able to distinguish yourself from every other individual in a world with a current population of nearly 8 billion? Knowledge of self will help you stand out from the rest of the pack. That said, the practice of Hoodoo requires you to take things a step further. You need to know your roots. Your ancestors are your roots; those who came before you, those with whom you share a blood connection.

Of all of the forms of magic available, blood magic is considered to be the most powerful, the most potent and the most dangerous. Blood contains a direct link to the people who came before you. In a scientific sense, your history is written in your blood. This is how science is able to connect your DNA with your blood relatives, and this DNA can be traced back generations. Ancestral magic goes beyond blood. It refers to the essence left behind by those who came before you. You came from someone who came from someone who came from someone and so on. Acknowledging this lineage connects you to the power of this linkage.

The truth is that whether you acknowledge your ancestry or not, there is always a possibility that you are paying for something that your ancestors did. It could be good or it could be bad. Their actions, inactions, spoken words and emotions all flow through anyone who is a part of their lineage. Ever met a person with an uncontrollable temper? Look into the person's lineage and you may find that there is someone who actually exhibited those traits.

This is why some people tend to experience an unusual amount of luck. It is not because lady luck is standing over their shoulder. Instead, there is every chance that their ancestors did something that brought about a reward that is being passed from one generation to the next. Unfortunately, the opposite is also the case. If your ancestor is known to have committed an offence so grievous and grave that it attracted a curse, this curse might be transferred to their descendants. Even beyond the transference of curses and blessings, there is power linked to our lineage. Failure to acknowledge this power weakens its potency over time, until it feels almost non-existent.

That doesn't mean that the power is suddenly extinguished. It remains dormant until you awaken it by acknowledging your ancestry. Think of your bank account. When you continuously carry out transactions with that account, it remains active but when you leave it for a long period of time, it gradually becomes dormant. The account is not closed, but is simply inactive. Ancestral spirits guide us because they see things that we do not see. They have experienced things that have happened before and, as they say, history has a way of repeating itself. Who else is in a better position to prevent you from repeating the mistakes of your past, if not an ancestor? Also, when it comes to rituals that require their help, a spirit with a direct link to you is usually more willing to provide assistance than one that is merely drifting. Consider all of these factors and understand them before you proceed.

To show your respect for your ancestors, consider setting aside a portion of your home for them. An ancestral altar is an important place in Hoodoo, because it's a place to invite your ancestors into your life. You can use your altar to call on them for not just aid in your magic, but for advice about your life. A small table is a fine place for an altar. If you have pictures of your ancestors, you can place these on the table, along with a glass of water. You might even leave offerings of food or alcohol, like whiskey or rum, every week, if you wish.

The Spirits of Roots

The practice of Hoodoo was originally called Rootwork, because the bulk of Hoodoo practice centers around the use of roots and herbs for both physical and spiritual aid. For example, if you are having a chronic headache, there are plants that you can use to treat that headache. If you need to bring luck into your life, there are roots that can help with that as well.

Before humankind fell in love with science and technology, we had a deep connection to nature. Part of that fundamental connection to nature was our relationship with plants. By utilizing plants in specific ways for unique spells, you are able to tap into the spirit within that plant to create the results you desire.

We have always known that plants can help provide a connection between our minds, bodies and spirits. Some plants are blessed with the unique ability to break the veil between our world and the spirit world. They allow you access to the other world, where you can reach out to the spirits and receive direct answers to your problems.

There are roots that can draw love or luck, protect you from evil and keep unwanted people away. There are roots to help you get a job or a promotion, roots to cleanse your spirit and cleanse your home. Knowing which roots do what is crucial if you ever want to do more than buy commercial love spells.

Much like words, roots have nuances. There are many roots that can draw love, but it's important to know which one you should choose and for which occasion. Coriander draws fidelity in love, while ginger adds passion and heat. Grapevine ties people together, lemon balm removes bad luck in love, and myrtle keeps love passionate in long-term relationships or marriages. There are many more roots for love, and the same kind of nuance applies in every other kind of spell.

The Spirits of Earth

In the opening of the first chapter of this book, I talked about a spell for attracting wealth in which I used earth that had been dug up near a bank. I used it because the energy of a place leaks into the ground around it, much like a sponge absorbing water. A bank is a place that draws money to it, and that money-drawing energy is transferred into the soil.

In the same way, you can use earth from near a hospital for healing, or earth from a casino to draw luck. Or you can use earth from the grave of an evil person to draw evil to someone else. Hoodoo is not all love and luck spells, after all.

In Hoodoo, we also add earth to magic spells to ground them, the same way electrical lines are grounded in the earth. Magic from roots or ancestors is powerful, but the strength of that power needs to be focused and controlled or you can end up with some unexpected results. Earth in a spell can stabilize it, calm it, and direct it where you want it to go. If I have a client asking for a spell to draw love into her life, I'll often add dirt from a church, so that the man we draw will be a good one. It's easy to draw love from the wrong man.

We all know that the earth is full of riches. When you think of precious stones and plants, in fact, you could say that the kind of wealth that the earth possesses is the most sustainable type of wealth. So it makes sense that when you include it in your spell and call upon the spirits of the earth, you draw on that wealth energy and divert it to your will.

It is for these reasons that you should try to be selective about the places where you obtain earth for your spell. For instance, if you take earth from a desert, the general idea is to attract dryness and barrenness. This is why, when placing curses, most practitioners go to places that symbolize what they want to visit upon the intended victim of the spell.

When carrying out any kind of spell, regardless of the elements or tools you will use, you must be very selective about what goes into it. Even the slightest mistake can alter the balance of the spell you are trying to create. So, when you choose earth, choose wisely. Understand its meaning. Try as much as possible to know its history before you use it. For the standard spells that I talk about in this book which require the help of earth spirits, I recommend going to places where the soil is rich and fertile. Places where you can see actual vegetation growing and thriving. As you continue to grow in the practice and craft of Hoodoo, you can expand your search to soils from other places.

Graveyards

Working Hoodoo in a graveyard is, honestly, not for beginners. Working with the spirits there requires a high degree of intuition that beginners usually don't have. Also, spirits in the graveyard can be dangerous. Just like walking into a strange neighborhood, some of the folks there may not be happy to see you and may wish you harm. I strongly suggest you get a good deal of experience working with your ancestral spirits, at home at your ancestral altar, before you move to working in a graveyard. However, I would be remiss in not at least discussing graveyards, because graveyards, and the spirits that live there, as such an important part of Hoodoo.

Graveyard magic is like combining the power of ancestral spirits with earth spirits. You can imagine how powerful this combination is. Many people associate a graveyard with sorrow and grief, or perhaps are just terrified of them, thanks to Hollywood movies. In Hoodoo, we do not share this perspective. In fact, death is not always regarded as the worst thing that can happen. Neither is it seen as an entirely negative experience. Of course, we hope that the people we love will always be with us in physical form, so losing them causes us pain. But because we also understand that there is a world beyond ours, where death is a bridge, we simply view death as the end of one journey and the commencement of another.

Graveyard magic is powerful, but maybe not for the reasons you think. Graveyard earth is used because it is a place of transition; of endings and beginnings. So if you are looking to end a cycle in your life that has proven to be very disruptive and destructive, graveyard earth might be just what you need. Also, if you have a relationship that has taken its toll on your mental and physical health, you might want to consider graveyard earth.

But it can also be used to herald new beginnings. The end of one thing often means the beginning of something new. If you find yourself in a place where you are about to start something new and you need something to initiate and activate the blessings associated with this new phase, graveyard earth might be the best option for you.

I should point out here that, just as you should be selective about where you get your earth, you should also pay close attention to the particular cemetery or grave from where you got your earth. If you go to a grave where the deceased was a dangerously psychotic person, you risk introducing very unstable elements into the spell you are trying to create.

When going to graveyards to collect grave dirt, you must be respectful. It is important to appease the spirits whose earth you are taking for your spell. You should always pay for the dirt you take, either by burying a few pennies or spilling some whiskey on to the ground. And because of how strange it looks for others to see someone digging around a cemetery for earth, I have learned over the years to do it under the guise of planting new flowers by grave sites.

To find a spirit to work with, you can use a method of divination like cards or a pendulum, but I usually work by instinct and intuition since I've been doing this for a long time. Walk around the graveyard, taking your time to get a feel for the place and the spirits that live there. Eventually you may feel pulled to one grave in particular. Before you strike up a conversation, I suggest doing some research about the person who was buried there, if you can. Were they a good person in life? A mother, a father, a nurse, a gambler? I'll say it again – spirits can be dangerous. Do your research.

If you've found a spirit you want to try working with, start off with an offering. Use your intuition or divination technique to get a feel for what the spirit might want, be it alcohol or food or cigars. Strike up a conversation and learn to listen to what the spirits have to say. Do not go into this kind of relationship with transactional mindset. Try and make a friend. Later, days or weeks later, you can ask your friend for a favor, or if you can take some of the dirt from their grave.

Crossroads

Where two roads cross, possibilities open up. In Hoodoo, we visit crossroads for spells to open roads to new opportunities, and to rid ourselves of things we don't want in our lives, like bad luck or bad people. In Hoodoo, crossroads are associated with the beginning of a journey. Therefore, they are mostly used in protection spells. Like the graveyard, a crossroads symbolizes transition. The main difference is that it doesn't carry that grim connotation of endings.

There are places here in Louisiana where, when you arrive at a crossroads, you'll find by the corner of the road sacrifices or offerings. This practice is also common in parts of Africa, where the traditional form of Hoodoo is practiced. A crossroads is also considered the perfect place to dispose of the remnants of the spell that you created. This is because a crossroads is a neutral place in magic, generally speaking. So, if you have created something that was previously very potent and you would like to neutralize its power, you can take the leftovers from that spell and place it at a crossroads. With each day that passes, the power will diminish.

Spells involving crossroads are best performed late at night or early in the mornings. I suggest you have this at the back of your mind when you want to carry out such spells. For maximum effect, some people would advise that you go during the moments between midnight and the following day.

Finding Balance

When you are preparing a meal, one of the first things you try to achieve in the process is a balance of flavors. This is because you are bringing a lot of different ingredients together and each of these ingredients has their own unique flavor. If you fail to pay attention to how those flavors complement each other, some might overpower others. This will likely either ruin or at least negatively affect the taste of the food. The same principle can be applied when creating a spell. You have to be fastidious about ensuring that you are creating a balance of powers. You cannot allow one power to overwhelm another, because it would impact the results. It doesn't matter how seemingly simple the spell is. You must be conscious of the elements involved in the creation and development of that spell.

Some spells will require the use of items that may come with a lot of power, especially if they have not been blessed, cleansed or if the previous owner was mentally unstable and left a residue of their essence on the item. When you add this into you spell, you are already tipping the balance. You'll need to find other ingredients that will either even out or counteract the power that will be drawn from this artifact.

Earlier, I mentioned that earth is a stabilizing power, and so its use helps to ground spells and create balance. But this is not always enough, especially if you are unsure about the source of the earth you are using. Every Hoodoo practitioner, whether a beginner or an expert, must endeavor to master the tools of balance. Hoodoo channels things outside our realm and this means that we are often tiptoeing on the edges of things outside our consciousness.

This is why some Hoodoo experts will tell you that certain spells will leave you teetering on the edge. If you miss a single detail, no matter how little, it can tilt the balance and the outcome can be disastrous. I know that when you started this journey, you had the idea of creating simple spells to cause little changes that will impact your daily life. That is perfectly okay. But it does not exempt you from the responsibility of striving to maintain balance.

Another way to look at it is this; with each spell that you create, you are absorbing energy from one dimension and leaving an empty space in its place. Using tools at your disposal, you should try to ensure that the energy you have removed does not create chaos on the other side that could lead to problems in later life.

Purification and Cleansing

Cleansing and purification rituals are not unique to any religion or spiritual practice. They are done across the board. Whether you are a Christian, a Voodoo practitioner or a Buddhist, there are purification exercises that you must undergo that will open you up spiritually. This is also true with Hoodoo. Beginners often dive straight into a spell without carrying out this purification stage. If you were learning under a Hoodoo teacher, a cleanse and purification ritual would be one of the first things you would be taught, because it is vital to the process. It cleanses you mentally, emotionally and physically, and then opens you up spiritually for the next stage of your journey. Taking a spiritual cleanse does not mean you are physically dirty. It might just be an indication that you are tainted by something beyond your control and closed off to the desires that you want to manifest in your life.

With the right tools, ingredients and elements, you can create a spiritual opening that will allow you access to these blessings. Now, contrary to the image that a cleansing bath or purification ritual conjures, you will not be slipping into perfumed herbs and oils in a warm bathtub with scented oils and candles surrounding you. Instead, what usually happens is a methodical dumping of powerful herbs and potions onto your body to achieve the clinical objective of opening you up spiritually. But fortunately, the effect of a cleansing ritual is almost immediate. You can sense it the moment it happens. The way it happens depends on what your objectives for the rituals are. For example, if your objective is to make yourself more receptive to love because you are planning a love spell, the cleansing process will start from your feet upwards. If the goal is to ward off negativity, the cleansing process works in the opposite direction, from your head downwards.

It is also worth noting that you must pay attention to the timing of this ritual. It must be done before the sun rises. Do not do it as the last item on your to-do list before you go to bed. Also, make sure that you do not speak to anybody before you carry it out. Wake up before sunrise, begin the process and carry out the routines associated with it. It will be over sooner than you expect. At the end of a cleansing bath, the water should not be drained from the tub as it is when you take a regular bath. Instead, if you are trying to attract something into your life, take the water containing the remnants or residues of the spell and toss it towards the east, where the sun rises. But if you intend to ward off something, by creating a protection spell, for example, the remnants of this water must be tossed at a crossroads.

I will go into more details of the cleansing and purification rituals in a later chapter. For now, these are the basics with which you need to familiarize yourself. Read up as much as you can on the subjects that I have discussed in this chapter. Master what you need to learn and ensure that you are conscious of the mandate that you have been given; to ensure that a balance is maintained at all times. Now I think you are ready for the next stage, which is Rootwork.

4

ROOTWORK

As I noted earlier, an alternative name for Hoodoo is 'Rootwork', because so many of the spells and magic conjured have a connection to plants. I also explained the role that the plant spirits play in the casting of a spell. I talked about the belief that certain spirits inhabit plants, and so each plant has unique attributes that can influence the outcome of the magic you wish to create. Across every culture, plants have been known to possess healing properties, but in Hoodoo, or Rootwork, if you prefer, things are taken a step further. Here, the plants are utilized beyond their physiological markers. In this chapter, we'll explore this concept in its entirety at a beginner level, and you'll develop a basic understanding of the symbolism of specific herbs, as well as some of the best practices in Rootwork that will help you produce or even amplify the desired results.

Basic Instructions on Roots

When it comes to the instructions about using roots, the first place to start is with your intention. If you intend to simply dabble in a few spells to meet some of your short-term needs, it is okay to pop into the store, pick up the things you need and begin casting. However, if you want to be a proper Hoodoo practitioner, you must understand the role that Earth plays in the empowerment of the plants with which you will be working. You should get used to the idea of either having your very own herb garden or learning to be a gatherer. The reason is simple; the herbs you pick yourself are still very much connected to Earth, which we know is a powerful component when it comes to the creation of Hoodoo magic. That is not to suggest that the plants you purchase in the store will not give you acceptable results. For basic spells and, even in some cases, advanced spells, store-bought plants can be very effective. But if you want something that is spiritually enriched, sustainable and in alignment with our practices, you must learn to interact with nature. There is something deeply satisfying about reaching into the soil, nurturing a plant from its seed days to the point of harvest, and then taking that plant from the soil to your potion, or whatever it is you want to use it for.

Before you strap on your boots and head into the wild to forage for herbs, though, I urge you to do some research. This will help you to differentiate between the many types of herbs. My grandmother started by teaching me which ones were edible and which ones were not. As a beginner, there are common herbs you should have in your garden. Growing them does not require a large space or a great deal of maintenance. You can grow them in pots or recycled bottles and still enjoy the benefits that come with this process. The most common herbs used in Rootwork are sage, rosemary and mint. You can continue to expand this list as you become better at recognizing and growing them. One of the reasons I love having my own herb garden is the easy access it gives me to the plants I use in my potions and mojos. Because they are readily available to me, I am able to create mixes in my home that will enhance the atmosphere for creating magic at the drop of a hat. For instance, it is generally believed that sage is a cleansing plant that can be used to ward off evil. Imagine days when you feel that there is a lot of negative energy in your space. During the time it takes you to purchase what you need from the store, that energy is creeping into every corner of your home. When you have your own garden, you can simply dash out and pull up what you need, then put the right ingredients together and immediately begin the ritual.

If growing the herbs yourself does not sound appealing to you, the next best thing is to work with people who grow them for Hoodoo purposes. Most people who grow herbs for magical purposes are well-educated on the art and craft behind it. For example, they usually plant these herbs according to the moon cycle, which is believed to empower the plants with even greater magical properties. The timing of their harvest is also crucial, as certain plants are said to bloom and reach their magical peak at midnight during full moons. So, when you buy from a recognized magical herb dealer, you can be certain that you are getting the highest quality that will deliver the best outcome. Again, you can go to the store to get what you need for basic spells but I suggest you begin to see plants as more than just things that grow from the earth. If you are going to be a Hoodoo practitioner, you must understand the place of roots/plants in creating magic.

Root Capabilities

In this section, I will focus on just 10 of the more common herbs that we deal with. These herbs will be featured in many of spells throughout the book and I will also share quick tips on how you can use them even without an active spell or potion. Remember, if you want to get the most out of them, buy them from someone who grows them for magical purposes or else grow them yourself.

Alfafa: This is a plant commonly used to attract money. As a practitioner, if you have a few of these in your home, it will help to ensure that money is always in your house. You can also sprinkle a bit of it in your wallet or pocket to attract money into it.

Angelica root: This particular root will keep dark and negative forces at bay. If you are a woman, you can use this to amplify your femininity and can also utilize it to create protection spells for your children. I also have a few beginner spells that use the power in Angelica root to attract luck.

Black Mustard Seed: We also call this "the seed of strife," because its primary purpose is to create confusion in the mind of your enemies. If you have a dispute with someone who is constantly troubling you, sprinkling some black mustard seeds on the path where they are known to walk can stir up confusion that will destabilize them and throw them off your path.

Chamomile: In general herbal medicine, chamomile is believed to have a calming effect and is good for people who have sleeping problems. In Hoodoo magic, you can use this to neutralize spells that you think have been cast against you.

Dandelion root: If you ever have a spell where you need to draw on help from your ancestors, using a dandelion root can amplify your reach and connection, making it easier to access them. If you are having trouble sleeping and feel that you are the victim of spiritual attacks, using dandelion in some of the potions that I will share in this book can help provide additional protection and will help you sleep better.

Fennel: Ensure your home is a safe space, free of bad spirits and negative energy that might corrupt the magical atmosphere, by hanging fennel seeds on your windows. If you need a little dose of courage for something, putting fennel seeds in your pocket can help. When I first started casting spells myself, I used to have fennel seeds in my pocket or in my palm to give me extra confidence. I encourage you to do the same.

Ginger: Until you become an advanced Hoodoo practitioner, I advise you to chew a little bit of ginger before you cast a spell. It is one of those herbs with an "amplifying" ability. Another effective use of ginger root is in spells that are used to increase desire in a relationship. But in a general sense, it is used to attract success.

Hibiscus: Warding off dangerous spirits is very important in the practice of Hoodoo magic, but at the same time you need to connect with the right spirits. Using the hibiscus plants in specific spells can attract good spirits that will, in turn, be happy to help you achieve your goal. You also use this in spells that are related to love, marriages and relationships.

Lemongrass: If you feel that you are suffering from a curse or that you have been jinxed, some of the cleansing spells and baths that I will talk about in this book use lemongrass to wash away the negative effects of those curses or completely neutralize the jinx.

Mandrake root: This is a multipurpose plant that can be used for different spells and rituals. It can be bound to a doll and used for a love spell. It can be inserted into a mojo bag to either attract money or repel evil forces and is also commonly used in fertility potions.

Root Spells

The list of herbs provided above are just some of the most basic herbs you should keep in your home. I want to point out that herbs are not the only things used in creating spells. It is called Rootwork, of course, but other non-plant-related elements, such as bones and stones are essential for the preparation of certain spells.

You will find that many different roots and herbs are used in creating attraction spells to empower you or provide protection. You either want to attract wealth, luck or love or you are seeking to empower yourself emotionally by raising your confidence level, or want to protect yourself from negative energy, negative spirits and potential curses. Most of the spells that will be performed in this book, and that you will perform as you grow in the craft, will center around these needs. And that is why it is important that you learn about roots at this early stage.

There are a lot of online resources that can help teach you the different kinds of herbs that are used in Rootwork. We would need a whole second book if I were to go into all of them. But for now, I am covering what you need to know as a beginner. The next step, as I mentioned earlier, is to learn how to properly identify and differentiate between herbs. Some plants look alike, so you need to smell them in order to determine which is which. The final step is to learn what herbs to mix together and what not to mix. It is easy to assume that simply because they are plants, they can all go together without consequences. Creating a spell is very different from creating a salad. You are not relying on the flavor of the plant. Instead, you must assess the energy, and certain energies clash. When you have a clash of energy in a potion, it either nullifies the desired effect or amplifies a negative outcome.

My reason for adding this caution here is not to scare you but to help you understand that you are not dealing with ordinary elements and materials. You are dealing with a magical force and you have to practice your spell creations with respect for the craft. Take the time to learn and grow as a Hoodoo practitioner. Use the foundation that this book will provide as a stepping stone to your next stage in Hoodoo practice. Call on your ancestors for guidance because, yes, they are always willing to provide assistance. Some of the spells I know today were not handed down to me directly from Mama Estelle. I intuitively knew what to put together and I believe that that was as a result of my connection with my ancestors. They guided me through the process and yours are always willing to guide you if you open up to them. One way to open yourself up to your ancestors is by cleansing yourself. The spiritual cleanse is a vital part of a spell-casting process and we will get into that in the next chapter.

5

SPIRITUAL CLEANSING

"Purify me with hyssop and I shall be clean.
Wash me and I shall be whiter than snow"
Psalm 51:7

For a brief moment, let us remove magic from the equation and focus on the emotional, mental and psychological benefits of having a bath. When, after a long, hard day, you come home and immerse yourself in a bath with your favorite soaps and scents, regardless of your gender, it has an uplifting effect on the psyche. Now, if you turn this experience up a notch by including herbs imbued with specific powers, you can amplify the effect of a cleansing bath on your spirit and even on your physical well-being. If you have been paying attention, you have noticed that I use the word "amplify" a lot. This is not a coincidence or a grammatical addiction. It is because I believe that this word is exactly what Hoodoo practice is all about. You are taking what naturally exists and harnessing its power to increase your chances of achieving the outcome you desire. So, forgive me for using this word a lot. In time, you will understand why. For now, let us take a closer look at purification baths, cleanses and the rituals associated with them.

Purification Baths: Symbolism and Application

Purification baths are meant to purify you for the ritual you want to perform and open you up spiritually to create a channel that allows you access to the spirit world, where you can make your petition known. By doing so, purification baths increase the chances of your desires becoming reality. But beyond opening you up, a purification bath serves other purposes, and I want to talk about a few of these right now.

Severing Ties:

Some of us unwittingly get ourselves into sticky situations, either through love ties, ancestral curses or as a result of our own actions. One of the many ways to get rid of such a tie is to undergo a purification bath. It helps to separate you from that person, curse or consequence. When it comes to soul ties, it is possible you will come across an individual who is unnaturally addicted to you. Their obsession with you might have negative repercussions in your life. Even if they are not doing anything spiritual, the fact that you may have had some kind of physical interaction with them, whether through intercourse or some other shared intimate activity, may have created a tie with

that person without you realizing it. These bonds can become dangerous, especially when the person becomes obsessed with you. As for
the ancestral curse, there are times when the sins of the father are
visited on the son, so just because you were born to this particular
individual could mean that you carry some pain and hurt in your
present life as a result of that lineage. There are special baths that you
can prepare to break such a tie and make sure that it ends perma-
nently. Finally, when you offend someone and that person holds a
grudge against you, if they are the spiritual type, they could engage in
declarations, sometimes through incantations and spells, that will
negatively affect you. Putting yourself through a purification bath will
separate you from those declarations and free you from the consequences.

For Protection:

As you ascend in your journey as a Hoodoo practitioner, one of the
things you will come to realize is the fact that a lot of the things we
deal with on a daily basis are more spiritual than they are physical.
The energy that people project towards you can affect you without
you even realizing it. The spaces that you inhabit are not entirely new,
as they belonged to previous owners. These people may have left a
very negative aura in that space, and if you do not perform a purification bath, you will find yourself absorbing some of that negativity in
different areas of your life. A purification bath helps to give you additional protection against these unpredictable elements. We can never
predict the intentions of another, but a purification bath will protect
you from them. Think of it as boosting your immune system. You
might not yet be sick but by feeding your body with the right vitamins

and nutrients, you arm yourself against any disease that may want to invade your body. In the same way, there may not currently be any spiritual attack or negativity in your physical space, but to maintain that serenity and ensure that you are well-guarded against any future attacks, a purification bath will create a barrier that keeps such things out.

For Attraction:

Anything with the ability to repel the negative can also attract the positive, so if you are preparing yourself to attract certain events in your life, a purification bath is a good idea. With the right ingredients, you can use your body as a channel that attracts the kind of things you want to see in your life. There are stones and other elements that can be used for this very purpose in the preparation of a purification bath. If you are able to diligently follow through on some of the rituals I will share shortly, you can make yourself a magnet for wealth, love or even luck. The impact of attraction spells that call for purification baths is greater than simply manifesting what you desire. You can also attract positive energy so that you find yourself constantly associating with the people that you need in your life. The main thing to remember when performing a ritual of this sort is to ensure that your mind is clear and focused on what you want.

Internal Cleansing

In Hoodoo, the practice of carrying out an internal body cleanse has more to do with ensuring that you are in a better position to invoke or conjure the things you want. I use the word "cleanse" because it's something that a lot of us can relate to, but the appropriate term is purification. As you continue to learn more on this journey, you will find that the word "purification" will expand to accommodate concepts like anointing, blessing and consecration. An internal body cleanse requires the ingestion of certain mixtures and concoctions designed specifically for this process. The herbs used in these mixtures are meant to intensify your psychic connection and provide clarity of thought so that you are able to focus your mind and zero in on the specific thing about which you want to consult with your ancestors.

This is another part of Hoodoo practice that requires caution and consultation with those who know exactly what they are doing. Some of the herbs that I work with for jobs or preparations of rituals are not exactly meant for consumption, so you need someone who knows the ins and outs of the plants that you intend to use and how their inter-action with one another could impact you physically. Failure to comply with instructions given by the Hoodoo doctor you work with might result in a failure of the spell or even health complications, especially if you ingest the materials. As a beginner, I would advise that you skip the internal cleansing ritual until you have reached a point where you have more knowledge on the subject. Instead, opt for ready-made herbal bath mixes. These mixes are often created with a specific purpose in mind. Go for the one that matches the expectation that you have and follow the instruction to the letter.

Finally, you should know that doing an internal cleanse is not solely reliant on ingesting herbs. There are crystals and other curios you might be able to use for such purposes. In some spells, you can light a candle and use the power of visualization to draw in the energy you need for an internal cleanse. I usually tell my beginner students that this is a better route to take unless you are working with an experienced Hoodoo doctor. The practice of Hoodoo is relatively safe, but it is important that you don't take this for granted by disregarding basic instructions. You might end up in a situation that is far worse than what brought you there initially or attract the wrong kind of energy into your life. I share these warnings because the practice of Hoodoo is not a hobby or to be engaged in on a whim. It requires dedication, devotion and due diligence.

Keeping Negative Energy Away

Many of us need to maintain a personal space filled with positive energy. This is why I feel like the perfect introduction to a purification bath is one that is meant to repel negative energy. In this segment, I am going to teach you how to create your own purification bath using some of the more common herbs, like the ones I listed earlier, and a few others you will need to obtain. I will also walk you through the step-by-step process to completing this ritual. As you continue to practice this, you will absorb more spiritual insight and guidance on some other necessary steps you can take to create results that are unique to different situations. But for now, let us fill your space with positive energy that will allow you to thrive spiritually and that will create a more enabling environment for your spells to work.

Duration:

This ritual takes place over a period of three days, so make sure you arrange your schedule to work without interruption. I would recommend that you do this once a month or once every quarter, depending on your experiences and personal needs. The first bath is meant to happen just after sunset. It is believed that this is the period that nega-tive forces begin to assemble. So the first ritual is going to be made up of bitters herbs that repel the activities and intentions of negative spirits towards you. The second bath is meant to be performed just before dawn and it is meant to attract positive energy. The third bath is much like the second and its sole purpose is to reinforce your inten-tions from that second bath. It acts as a seal for the attraction magic you are trying to create.

Preparation:

For the first ritual and the first bath on the first day, you will need the following:

- Dandelion roots
- Yarrow
- Wormwood
- Nettle
- Red or purple colored petals
- Horehound
- Vinegar
- Ammonia

It doesn't matter if the herbs used are fresh, dried or powdered. Remember that this is not a sexy bath situation, so don't try to do the whole spa-like treatment. Start by setting the hot water in the bathtub at a temperature that is hot but not so hot that it scares you, then add the herbs and petals into the hot water. Add 1/2 cup of vinegar and a few drops of ammonia and you are set.

For the second and third day of the week will you will need the following:

- Angelica
- Chamomile
- Hyssop
- Allspice
- Comfrey leaves
- Powdered Nutmeg
- Powdered Cinnamon
- White petals
- Honey
- Milk
- Egg

Again, the herbs used here can be fresh, dried or powdered. In addition to the powdered nutmeg and cinnamon, you can throw in some whole nutmegs if you have them. The milk should be three cups, and one egg is enough. I should also point out that you have to prepare the herbal mixture from scratch on the second and third day. Do not use leftovers!

Process:

Day 1: When the time is right, begin by filling the tub with hot water. Then take two candles (preferably white) and place them on opposite ends to act as a doorway to the bath. You will walk through this doorway to enter into the bath when it is ready. Next, pour the herbal mixture into the water along with the ammonia and vinegar, remove your clothing and enter the doorway you made with the candles. If you are using fresh or dried herbs, you can place them in an organza bag to prevent your tub from clogging. If you are a woman on your period, do not take this bath. Blood interferes with the magic. Wait until it's over before you engage in this ritual. Once you are in the water, focus your mind on whatever negative circumstances you are going through and imagine the positive outcome that you desire. Completely immerse yourself in the bath water.

Dunk yourself in the water at least seven times. Do not ingest the contents of this water. Each time you emerge, spend a few minutes meditating on the positive outcome that you desire in your life. If you are in a situation where you are attached to something negative, like bad debts, a bad relationship or just bad experiences that happened to you, use these meditation moments to detach yourself emotionally from those feelings. By the seventh time you emerge, the water should begin to feel cooler. Step out of the tub through the doorway that you created with the candles. Take a cup and scoop the contents of this water. Set it aside and drain the rest. Do not dry yourself. Allow the water and herbs to seep into your skin so that the magic can work. When you feel dry enough, put on your robe, take that cup of water that you extracted and go outside. Turn your face towards the West, hold the cup over your head and say these words: *"Whatever hold the negative forces or spirits have over me has been broken. I am free from every negative bond. As I cast this water over my head, I am also casting out every negative spirit and energy in my life."* After reciting these words, toss the water out and go back inside. You are done for the night.

Day 2 and Day 3:

Cleanliness is a requirement for these next two rituals, so it is important that you take a personal bath before you commence. Also ensure that the bathtub you use is very clean. Once you have done this, you can start the process by running hot water in the tub and lighting the candles to create an entryway. Next, crack the egg and drop it in the water before adding the herbals and the white petals and spices. Pour in the milk and honey and then enter the tub through the gateway you have created. The mixture has a sweet-smelling aroma. Enjoy this and allow it to inspire positive images in your mind. Dunk yourself in this water five times. As you emerge from each dip, feel yourself opening up to the positive energy in the world around you, as a petal opens up to the rising of the sun.

When you are finished, step out of the tub. With an empty cup, once again scoop out the contents of the bath water. If you used whole nutmegs, try to have at least one in the cup. Drain the rest of the water. Allow yourself to air dry and then step outside. This time, you will be facing the East. Instead of holding the water above your head, hold it close to your chest and say these words: *"I welcome this day with joy and gladness. I open myself to the blessings that the world has to offer me. I attract light, love and positivity to every area of my life. I welcome all the good spirits into my heart and into my home."* Toss the water in the direction of the rising sun. You feel like immediately washing off all that egg gunk in your hair but resist the urge. Give yourself time to absorb all the positive energy that the ritual has provided by waiting until you are completely dry. Personally, I don't wash off until the end of the day, when I have to prepare myself for the ritual the next day. But if you feel that you must wash off, do it after you are dry. If you successfully completed this ritual, congratulations! You have just performed your first authentic Hoodoo spell. How does it feel? If the magic excites you, wait until you create your first oil.

6

CONJURE OILS

Oils are another curious part of religion that have been used throughout the ages. You will find the use of oils in virtually all religions. In Hoodoo, oils are used as an accelerant, as well as a sealant. In other words, when you put a specific oil on an object or place or person, you are accelerating the power of the spell that you want to invoke or conjure within that object, place or person. You can also use it to seal that power that has been placed in/on them. For example, if you consecrate a specific place and assign it as holy, you need an oil to seal this consecration process. So whatever kind of spell you want to create, there is an oil mixture that can aid that process and that is what we'll talk about in this chapter. I will share the core uses of oil in Hoodoo and then highlight a spell that utilizes oils in its incantation.

. . .

Understanding Magic Powder and Oils

Powders and oils are an integral part of Hoodoo tradition. They have been used for centuries; long before it became commonplace to use essential oils for aromatherapy. The only difference between the general use of oils and the way they are used in Hoodoo practices is that each oil is conditioned with a purpose. This tradition is perhaps what gave rise to the knowledge that certain scents are associated with certain emotions and can invoke certain feelings. For example, the scent of citrus is said to inspire creativity. There is a lot of science that backs up the effectiveness of these aromatherapy oils. But as you well know by now, Hoodoo is not exactly science that can be cooked up in a laboratory. It requires the merging of mind and spirit.

Oils and powders are extracted from plants, and so, with the understanding of plant spirits and what they represent, you can extract the essence of that plant, combine it with other herbs in specific portions and then bind that to a purpose with your mind. It really is as simple as that. However, the process is very delicate. Therefore, it is important to pay attention to how these herbs are extracted and combined in order to achieve the results you want. More often than not, oils and powders can be used on their own without any additional magical components. So, let's say, for example, you wanted to attract wealth, or you are more specific about attracting money. There are oils and powders that have been crafted for this particular purpose. All you have to do is ensure that you are getting them from the right source and use as directed by the Hoodoo practitioner from whom you bought them and you are as good as gold. But if you want to be a

Hoodoo practitioner yourself, you will have to learn to create your own oils and powders.

While there are a lot of experts and people like myself who are deeply steeped in the practice of Hoodoo who can create the right oils for you, there is something beautiful about being able to create a mix that is unique to you. Eventually, as you advance and grow in the craft, you might be able to create these mixtures for other people as well. My goal and desire here is to pass on my knowledge to enable you to create your own herb mixes, oils and potions that are just as effective as mine, if not more so because they are specific to you. To create your own oil and powder mix, the first place to start is with the understanding of plants. Now you see why I said it is important to conduct research on all these herbs and plants. Don't just focus on their magical properties. You have to identify them individually. There are different species of each plant, which are unique to their geographical location. Mastering their uses and extraction process requires constant practice and study.

Because we have touched on the role that plants and plant spirits play in this kind of magic, I am going to focus on how to extract these plants to make oils or powders. But first we'll look at how to use these powders and oils.

How to Use Conjure Oils

Oils and powders are primarily used in anointing and dressing purposes. For example, if you want to attract money and you have a channel that can act as a doorway for that money to enter, you can use powders to ensure that that money comes to you by dressing that medium with the powder. Here is what I mean. Let us say you have a business where you sell specific products or services. Before sending the physical invoice to them, you might sprinkle some powder on the back of the invoice or on the envelope and then invoke a clear image of what your expectations are. I would think you would expect your client to pay on time and to continue to retain your services. With this thought clearly in your mind, gently lace the invoice as I mentioned.

When you have someone specific in mind to whom you want to direct your spell, powders can be an effective way to get the results you want. Simply sprinkle the powder in the area where they are likely to step. The potency of a powder like this depends on how well it latches on to that person's imprint, which carries their essence. One thing you will quickly learn about Hoodoo magic is that the essence of a person is a very important ingredient in increasing the potency of the spell that you are casting. This is because the spell in question is no longer generic, but instead has a unique identity to work with. Let us say you live in a neighborhood that is relatively quiet, except for one annoying neighbor who is a nuisance to you. A quick way to get them out of your life without having to tip the balance of good and evil is to use Hoodoo powder. Sprinkle this powder on a well-known path where they walk. Mixing the powder with a little bit of dirt will help disguise it. Once you have sprinkled it, you have to seal the spell with your intention by vocally saying their name and what you want to happen. There are specific powder mixtures that can act as a repellent and when you attach your intention to such a mixture, you are guaranteed to get results almost immediately. This can also work if you are trying to get attention from that person.

Oils work a little differently from powders, which has a lot to do with their consistency. For instance, if you sprinkle oil on an invoice, it would look tacky and you would come off as unprofessional. This bad impression that the image creates will set the mind of the recipient against you. So it is better to use powder in certain situations and oils in others. One instance where both oil and powders can be used is when you are creating a spell or working with candle magic. There are candles that are created for spell purposes. Sprinkle a little bit of powder or oil on the uppermost part of the area where the candle is burning and then place your intentions on that candle so that as it burns, the spell will be activated and cause your desires to manifest in your life. You can also use oils and powders as a way to feed your mojo bags. In the next chapter, we are going to be talking in greater detail about mojo bags. But the thing you need to understand about them right now is that their power wanes over time. For this reason, you need powders and oils to continue feeding that energy if you want to keep the spell active and relevant.

There are many other ways to use Hoodoo oils and powders, but I am saving some of those tips for the chapters where we get into the creation of spells, so you can see this part of Hoodoo practice in action. For now, the only thing left to discuss is how to create or conjure up your own magic oils and powders.

Creating Personalized Oils

Creating you own oils will require having a neutral carrier oil as your base. Personally, I like to use homemade coconut oil. It is a very receptive oil and adapts its structure to whatever herbal elements you put in it, so if you add herbs that are very strong, it will adjust its physiological nature and adopt the potency of whatever you are using. It is also soft enough to be flexible when you want something very mild. For love potions, I prefer to use oils extracted from flowers, like roses. The nature of the rose plant is very open to love, and when used in a spell it can invoke very strong imagery in the mind of the recipients. As a beginner, I would recommend the oils I have listed below. When you become stronger in the craft, you can move on to oils like berg-amot oil and so on. For your first lesson, the intention is to create a *"Get me a Job"* oil. These are hard times we live in and you might need a little spiritual boost to help you get ahead. For this oil, you will need the following:

- Allspice - Used in prosperity spells
- Cinnamon - Attracts luck
- Coconut oil - An excellent base oil
- Dill - To make you irresistible
- Sage - For wisdom and to ward off evil eyes

Use a transparent glass bottle for this work. Pour your base into this bottle or jar and then add the cinnamon, allspice, dill and sage. If you are using fresh dill and sage, you will need to prep them ahead of time by bruising the leaves a little before immersing them in oil. Let them sit in the bottle overnight and then pour the oil and herb mixture into a strainer. Squeeze to extract and then use what is in the container. Ensure that no fresh leaves get into the mixture. Repeat this for three days with new dill and sage leaves.

On the third day, you should have enough to use for the mixture. Put the allspice and cinnamon into the oil/herb mixture. Shake it and set it down for an entire day. For the next week, continue shaking it several times every day. At the end of the seventh day, you have your first magic oil. Rub this on the sole of your shoe before you go for a job interview. You are bound to get positive outcomes. Another way to amplify the potency of this oil is to use it on a candle. Hoodoo incantations involving candles are a special kind of magic close to my heart and I will tell you all about them in the next chapter.

7

MAGIC CANDLES

M agic candles are commonly used in Hoodoo practice. You will find them used by themselves in spells, or with other elements such as powders, oils and roots. Outside of Hoodoo magic, candles create a kind of light that enables you focus and draw on your psychic energy. When your psychic energy levels are elevated, you are able to project your thoughts and direct them accurately towards your intentions. This is why a lot of exercises that involve meditation call for the use of candles. It provides light but with a glow that resonates with your spiritual aura. The elements that are used in the creation of a spell are only one part of the equation meant to give you the magic that brings about the manifestation of that spell. The second part of that equation is your mind. Having a candle in that process will help center and focus your mind. This is why I love candle magic. No matter how confused or disoriented you feel, when you put a candle in the mix, your mind is brought to the center of the problem and distractions are eliminated, thus giving you the ability to effectively carry out your incantations. In this chapter, I want to further explore this process and concept.

The Power and Intent of One

The mind is a very powerful tool but at the same time it requires utmost discipline and sometimes spiritual intervention to focus on a singular problem. There are people who are gifted with the singular focus that is required in the creation of a magical spell. However, this gift is extremely rare and even those who have require years of practice to harness it. When you have an immediate problem to solve and you want to use magic to fix it, time is a luxury you cannot afford. But having a candle in the mix can help cut that time significantly because it draws your focus to its light and helps you bring your intentions and willpower into one place.

Even with the right portions of mojo bags, purification baths and herbal mixtures, a spell can go wrong if an untrained mind is behind its activation. You need to be in agreement with the spirit behind all the elements required for the spell. You have the herbs that are meant to attract what you desire in your life and you have taken the bath that has opened you up spiritually. Your mind is the final gateway that will introduce the manifestation of the magic into your life and this is why it has to be unified in its intent. This is not always easy. As you well know, life pulls us in different directions. Even when you are very certain that the decision you are about to make is the right one, there will usually be that voice of doubt that makes you feel as if there is something else you should be doing.

A lot of people complain about how the spells they cast were not effective, or the portions they bought from the Hoodoo doctors were fake and so on. Sometimes these complaints are valid. But the real reason behind the failure of the spell is often the absence of unification of the mind. You need to be at one with the magic of the elements you are using in the spell. You need to align your thoughts and willpower with those of the spirits that you will conjure up for the spell. Many people who have come to study under me had to first learn to adjust their mentality about magic. You see, the spirits, herbs and all these wonderful things from which we are drawing magic are not just lying dormant waiting for someone to control them. They are active forces on their own and can only be moved by people who have mastered their own minds. This little bit of information is especially important if you are dealing with the kind of spell that is designed to influence the will of another. I am talking about love spells, commanding spells and others like them.

Therefore, because of the technicalities involved in the creation of magic, it is important to introduce candles and learn how to work with them. Some candles are imbued with magical powers and they help to amplify your thoughts. Some are simply representing your intentions and they draw on your energy to boost the spell. Then there are candles that you bind to your purpose with special oils and herbs. Whatever type of candle you use, the objective remains the same; to unify your thoughts, your willpower and your desires with the magical intent of your heart. This is the key to unlocking the power of the elements.

· · ·

Colors and their Manifestations

Candles are shaped in different ways and this is deliberate. They have specific meanings that can help channel the magic you are trying to create in a certain way. This knowledge of the shapes of candles is something I think should be learned later on. As a beginner, your primary concern should be with the colors. Through technology, candles are being created in a greater variety of colors than we ever had in the early days. However, these different shades still fall into specific categories, so I am not going to focus on the range of colors in their different shades. Instead, I am going to start with the seven primary colors that are used in conjuring, Rootwork and magic. I will share the significance of the candles and explain what the color represents.

Black Candles: There is a general misconception that black candles are typically used for dark magic and deep-seated occult practices. While a part of this is true, black candles do not necessarily signify evil. In the world of Hoodoo magic, black is a protection color and so if you want to create a protection spell, a black candle would be most effective. If you also need a spell that involves dominance over the will of another person or entity, a black candle is a must. An example of such a spell would be a break-up spell or a banishing spell.

White Candles: Most purifying spells are done under the ethereal glow of a white candle. This is because white signifies purity, protection and, in many cases, peace. White is a deeply spiritual color that invokes harmony and a sense of calm. It is the traditional go-to color for most basic Hoodoo incantations. It provides clarity of thought and can help you center your focus if you are having trouble with it.

Red Candles: Red is a vibrant and passionate color and, as you can imagine, it a perfect color to use when the spell involves love. On the opposing end of this emotion is revenge, which can be dangerous. Red evokes powerful emotions and if you need a colored candle to stir up such emotions, you cannot go wrong with this one. Just be careful, though. As your feelings are being stirred up, you still need to maintain control and mastery over them. You don't want your feelings all over the place. This will only cause chaos with your spell.

Green Candles: Draw on the energy of money spirits with green candles. Green is also associated with vegetation, which means growth and prosperity. If the spell you are working on has to do with fertility, this is the right color of candle to use. Spells that have to do with luck, abundance and growth can draw energy from green candles.

Yellow Candles: Yellow is such a positive and upbeat color that even when it is used under the direst circumstances, it has a way of immediately brightening your mood. This candle is a personal favorite of mine. I usually light this when I am feeling down or depressed. Even without an active spell linked with it, the glow of the candle amplified by the color almost always cheers me up immediately. Unsurprisingly, it is used in spells that evolve around happiness, friendship and mental clarity.

Silver Candles: If the spell you are creating needs to draw on feminine energy, a silver candle is the surest way to get the results you want. Another interesting use of silver candles is to mirror moon magic. There are specific magic spells that need to be performed under the light of the moon. However, you would need to wait until that point in order to harness the moon energy. But in case of an emergency, lighting up a silver candle will cast a moonlit glow over the spell and improve its efficiency.

Blue Candles: Sharpen your communication skills under the light of a blue candle. Promote healing and sound mental health with spells cast in the glow of a blue candle. Using a blue candle is also excellent for meditation exercises. After carrying out a purification bath, I like to light a blue candle and meditate on the positive outcome I am expecting.

Candle Reactions

Candle reading is a Hoodoo practice that you will learn in time. When you light a candle and put it in a spiritual element, it draws on the energy in the environment and you can read the flames to interpret the energy in the space you are in. The art of candle reading is somewhat advanced because there is a lot of information to learn. At this stage, I will simply share what you need to know at this level. If you want more information, you will have to do a bit of online research on the topic. There are also books that will enlighten you about how to read candle flames. I am also considering writing a more advanced version of this book, so watch for that.

There are three basic things to look out for as a newbie Hoodoo practitioner. First, you look at the color of the flame, then the movement of the flame and finally the brightness of the flame.

. . .

Color Reaction

The power of the candle flame ranges from blue at one end of the spectrum to red at the other end, with yellow and orange in between. A blue flame is indicative of the presence of a friendly spirit, like an angel or a fairy or even a familiar ancestral spirit. A red flame, on the other hand, signifies the presence of a very powerful entity. Yellow and orange speaks of the presence of active energy that could be helpful in the spell.

Flame Movement

When candles flame, it is usually in the direction of the wind. But when you are in a closed space and the flame flickers, pay attention to what direction the flame is pointing towards. It will tell you the state of your spell. For example, an east-facing flame indicates mental soundness in the spell that you have created while a west-facing flame points to the strength of the emotion surrounding the spell. A north-facing flame is usually the result of a physical factor, while south-facing flames speak to the fact that your physical energy is powered by intent.

Flame Brightness

Candle flames burn at different levels. A low-burning flame might mean you need to up the energy levels required to push the spell forward. A flame that is burning bright and fast but unevenly means the spell is not grounded. You want a slow, steady burn that tells you your spell is going in the right direction.

8

MOJO BAGS

A mojo bag can be the most personalized form of magic. You use it to draw on powers that can be invoked in the spells that you create, in the daily activities that you carry out and also in your practice of Hoodoo. Everything you have learned up to this point was bringing you to this place where you learn how to create your own mojo bag. In this chapter, I will talk about what a mojo bag really is. I will also share some tips on how you can create your own personal mojo bag. Some of my tips will enlighten you on how to continuously activate the power of your mojo bag so that it remains potent for a very long time. This is one of the most exciting parts of this process, because you will see your magic begin to evolve and develop its own identity. The things that we learn from our ancestors provide a foundation for our growth but with practice, we are able to add our own individual ingredients to the mix to create a signature magical identity. When this happens, if you perform a spell, the energy that comes off of that spell will have your name written on it because it will be a marker unique to you. Doesn't that sound exciting? If this is something you look forward to, I promise you will enjoy this chapter immensely.

What are Mojo Bags?

In the general term, a mojo bag is your own personal talisman. It is regarded as an amulet. In other cultures and religions you will find references to it when it comes to protection. When I looked online to find out what people thought about a mojo bag, one definition I loved described a mojo bag as "a prayer in a bag." This is nice and somewhat fitting but in Hoodoo, it goes beyond that. A mojo bag in Hoodoo practice is a signature spell bound to you with immense power to drive a specific purpose over a long period of time. Unlike the standard spells, which basically go on errands for your desires, a mojo bag is tied to a core aspect of your destiny. For example, there are protection mojo bags designed to keep you away from anything that could possibly hinder your progress in life. This type of magic is not only about protecting you from evil spirits or those who want to harm you but is essentially about keeping you on track when it comes to your purpose in life.

There is a huge difference between the work of a protection spell and that of a mojo bag created for protection. One is like buying an alarm system for your home to notify you of imminent danger and enabling you to act to prevent that danger, while the other is like having a round-the-clock bodyguard who is knowledgeable about every form of defense so that if there is an attack, all you need to do is follow the instruction of this bodyguard. You see how distinctly different that is?

You also have mojo bags that focus on specific emotions, like love. If you desire a particular person and want to attract their attention and affection but feel that you are unable to do so the natural way, a mojo bag might be the only way for you to get those things in a sustainable way. This is because a regular love spell will do the initial work for you, but as soon as that work is done, it diminishes in power. A mojo bag, on the other hand, will continue to activate your desire for that person as long as you feed the power that backs it in order to keep it potent.

Mojo bags are powerful; from the way they are created to the way they are activated and the way they are fed. There are critical steps you must take and conditions that must be fulfilled in order to benefit from their power. Whether or not you are spiritually attuned, the second the power in your mojo bag begins to wane, you will feel its impact because that is how strong the energy is that it projects. Do not dabble lightly in the creation of a mojo bag. You want to ensure that there is a balance of energy in this process and that the spell you are working with is well-grounded. The potency of a mojo bag will amplify the intent you have for that spell and if you fail to get it right in the preparation stage, it will amplify the negative repercussions of that failure. So, always use caution when creating a mojo bag. But when you get it right, you will activate a supernatural energy so intense that it will almost be like having your own personal genie at your beck and call, particularly in the area for which the spell was meant. If, for instance, you created the mojo bag for protection, you will find yourself in ordinary situations where you are supernaturally guarded. In such situations, you will not be able to explain some of the unusual saves that you experience. Now that we have thoroughly explored what mojo bags are, let us look at how they can be used.

THE VARIOUS USES OF MOJO BAGS

Mojo bags have several uses but for this level of training and practice of Hoodoo, I will focus on only three of them. But before I cover the three main uses, I want you to think of mojo bags as your super-packed multivitamin supplements. They power up your life in many ways and can be personalized and adapted to suit your specific goals and objectives. Now let us look at the three uses of mojo bags.

1. To Activate the Power That Attracts Your Desires

If you have a burning desire to see something specific manifest in your life through a spell, a mojo bag is the perfect thing to give that desire and activated spell an extra boost. There are situations that call for more than just a one-time spell. And even if you go through a full ritual like a cleanse or purification bath, you might be required to do more. Now, instead of performing these spells or purification baths every other week, having a mojo bag dedicated to this spell will be enough to hold the power from the moment your spell is activated to the point where it manifests. It doesn't matter what that desire is for; whether you are attracting love, wealth, luck or simply trying to end a relationship with someone. A mojo bag will create an atmosphere that pulls the power required for the spell and then sustains it until that thing you desire has manifested.

. . .

2. To Power a Protection Spell

Even the most basic protection spell requires immense power, and as a beginner you might not be able to draw on those elements on your own. A mojo bag created specifically for protection will ensure that the protection spell you have cast over yourself remains active over a long period of time. Again, it doesn't really matter how powerful or how basic the spell is, if you are working with the right ingredients or Hoodoo doctor, you should be able to sustainably power up the spell. Long ago, mojo bags were mostly used as talismans. Essentially, this meant that they had the same duties as bulletproof vests on police officers. A mojo bag would absorb whatever negative energy was directed your way and threatened to cause you harm. In some cases, it can even redirect that negative force towards its origin. However, in very simple terms, it serves as a barrier between you and anything that intends to hurt you, whether physically or spiritually.

3. To Draw on Deeper Inner Strength

One of the things my grandmother taught me that has stayed with me all through my life is the knowledge that I am powerful. I am going to pass this gift on to you; you are incredibly powerful. The only difference between you and me is the wealth of information I have. This knowledge that has been passed down to me by my ancestors has equipped me with information that I have been able to use to my advantage. What is my point? You have a dormant power inside of you and a mojo bag can awaken it and tap into it to give you some of the results that you desire. For example, if you want to experience more confidence or more calmness in your life, you should not be looking to spirits for this. Instead, you should be able to awaken the god or goddess inside you and a mojo bag is the right tool to do exactly that. So, if you find yourself in a season that stresses you out, such as our current climate, having a mojo bag with you at all times can help you experience a calm and patience that may be unlike you but is perfectly natural at the same time.

Making Personalized Mojo Bags

One phrase I have used throughout this chapter in describing the mojo bag is how specific it is to a spell. But more than that, it is also unique and specific to you. This means that your mojo bag cannot be used by another person. You also cannot allow someone else to see, touch or know about it. It is meant to be kept in a safe place on your person at all times. It can be made from a combination of herbs, stones and oils. But the most powerful ingredient is your intent. On that cheery note, let us create your first mojo bag. For this exercise, we are creating the inner peace mojo bag. You will need to gather the following items:

- A flannel bag in indigo blue
- A seashell
- A lapis lazuli stone
- Chamomile
- A peace symbol (optional)

Indigo blue is a color that calls on inner peace. This is why it is a perfect choice for this mojo bag. A seashell connotes the soothing and calming presence of the ocean during its gentle moments, and drawing on that presence is a great way to feed the energy you want to direct into this mojo bag. The lapis lazuli stone connotes harmony and tranquility and its potency in fulfilling the magic required for this makes it an excellent addition. Finally, throw in some chamomile seeds for that extra calming touch. Put these ingredients into the flannel bag and seal it with a peace symbol, if you like. I am particularly fond of the ohm sign, because it represents inner calmness. Find a symbol that you feel reflects what you want and then complete your mojo bag magic by placing your intent on it.

Hold the bag in your hands and speak what you desire. Your words could be something like this: "I experience calmness every time this bag touches me. I automatically relax and feel stress leaving my body every time I make contact with the bag. I never lose touch with this calmness that I have on the inside so that even in the most trying situations, I am able to keep my head above water. This is my intent and I speak it into action every single day of my life." Breathe on the bag so that it absorbs your essence and begins its cycle. Every other week, rub this mojo bag with an anointed oil to keep and sustain the power behind it and, just like that, your first mojo bag is activated.

With your first mojo bag creation, you have finished the basic training on your journey to becoming a Hoodoo practitioner. What you need now is a couple of spells for different situations to help you get started and to develop the knowledge you have right now. We will kick things off with some fundamental love spells.

9

SPELLS FOR LOVE

Love is a beautiful and pure emotion. It is such a great feeling to love and be loved at the same time. However, when this mutual love does not occur, but it is something you desire, especially when you have someone particular in mind, you might need some kind of spiritual intervention to trigger the emotion in the other person. From a logical standpoint, it's easy to understand why many struggle with love potions. It seems like a potion is meant to compel someone to do something that they don't want to do. But in reality, magic, especially Hoodoo magic, simply creates an opportunity that might not have existed before.

A person's emotions and feelings are not exactly being compelled against their will, although it's true that there are dark forms of magic that will channel that sort of energy. But in this case, an opportunity is presented for the seed of love to be sown. The person for whom the spell is intended is conscious of their willpower in the process.

Imagine this scenario. You are pining for someone who doesn't even know you exist. You have nothing but good will and good intentions towards them, but you have no idea how to initiate a romance. Performing a love spell is not going to suddenly make them fall in love with you. On the contrary, it merely creates an opportunity for them to see you in a different light. What happens from then on is up to them. Now let's look into simple Hoodoo love spells and learn how to create them.

The Place of Love Spells in Hoodoo

The subject of love spells or magic associated with love has been a source of controversy in many circles because of the ethics involved. But as I explained earlier, traditional love magic does not compel a person against their will. The spell is not designed to make a person fall in love with you. It is meant to create the circumstances that will provide opportunity and enhance an atmosphere for love to blossom. In fact, I like to think of love spells as creating an ambience that attracts genuine love but also the attention of the person on whom you are fixated.

Think of a love spell like an advanced flirting technique, but in this case you are not using words, body language or other tactics to show this person that you are interested in them. Instead, you are empowering the forces in your environment to provide the right signals that will welcome this love into your life. Of course, it would be unfair of me to not acknowledge the existence of dark magic that compels a person against their will. But the truth is that love spells are not the only spells in which a person's will is being subjected to that of another. There are spells designed to rob a person of their wealth or opportunity, and there are spells for vengeful reasons.

I am aware of these spells, but I do not use them because the idea repulses me, and also because there are negative repercussions. When you willfully subdue a person's willpower and impose your intentions on them, you create an atmosphere that attracts negative forces, which can build over time to the point where they become uncontrollable. Once that happens, you will find yourself regularly attracting negative circumstances into your life. I promise you it is not worth it.

In the next segment, I am going to talk about some things that you should never ignore, especially when it comes to love spells. It is better to err on the side of caution and walk on the path that is good.

Warnings You Must Never Ignore

When creating love spells, you must never ignore your own emotions that are attached to the spell you are creating. If your intentions are not out of love or genuine desire for good towards the person to whom the spell is directed, you will not have peace of mind. You will experience a sense of wrongness about the spell and once that sets in, you will receive a clear message from your subconscious that what you are doing is not appropriate. Whenever you sense this feeling, whether it is for a love spell or not, I urge you to stop. Look for other alternatives. The problem could be that the spell you want to cast is not the right one or that your intentions are not clear enough to activate the power you are seeking.

Another sign you must not ignore when creating a love spell is if you sense that the feeling this person has towards you is not genuine. It is possible that you have already had some kind of interaction with the person for whom the spell is intended but it did not move towards love. If that's the case, it might be an indication that this person does not feel the same way about you as you do about them. If you sense this, a spell will no longer be directed at creating opportunities but will instead work with the intention of forcing them to fall in love with you, which is not right. You should also watch for behavior that points towards an addictive personality. If the person has a history of drug or alcohol abuse, you should probably back away from the spell because if the right atmosphere is created, it could enhance their addictive tendencies and push that love emotion they have for you towards obsession, which of course is something you do not want.

Finally pay attention to their mental health. A person who has a history of mental health problems or who struggles with emotions like depression, anxiety and so on is not an ideal candidate for a love spell. Do not allow your own feelings to cloud your judgment. Watch for signs of these mental or emotional traits and have the decency to hold off creating a spell, because it will only complicate things for both of you.

POTENT LOVE SPELL RECIPES

There are five different types of love spells that I will share with you. Each of them is unique and serves a different purpose, as you will see. They can often be created using simple ingredients around the home but you may need to expand your search for some important ingredients:

Spell One: Come My Way Orange

Purpose: To create an atmosphere around you that acts as a magnet and attracts love

For this spell, you will need the following ingredients:

- Orange
- Rose
- Pins (Nine of them)
- Red thread
- A lock of your hair
- Follow Me Boy oil (I will share the recipe for this)

First, anoint the lock of your hair, the pin and the thread with the "look me over" oil. Then insert the lock of hair into the rose petal. Use a small carving knife to drill a hole into the orange. Insert the rose with the lock of your hair into this hole. Use the pins to close the hole and then weave the thread between the pins in order to "lock it." Bury this orange somewhere close to your phone and wait for love interests to begin to pour in. Always remember to keep your intent close at heart when you are creating a spell like this.

Spell Two: Call Me Hand

Purpose: To make someone specific contact you

Since you've probably attracted several love interests, it is possible that some have your phone number but have not reached out. This spell will help initiate the next phase. Like the previous spell, it is easy and can be done right in your kitchen. Here is what you will need:

- Licorice root
- A dime (mercury dime for something more potent)
- A paper with the name of the person on it
- A purple cloth

Wrap the dime and the licorice root in the paper that has the name of the person you want to call you. Wrap this paper in the purple cloth. Make your intentions known by calling out the person's name and saying, "I want you to call me." When you have done this, put it all on the floor and stomp on it. Do this nine times every day for nine days. Expect positive results.

Spell Three: Love Me Dearly Mojo Bag

Purpose: To increase the love that someone feels for you

This is the perfect spell if you have a love interest whose affection you want to boost to sustain the relationship. You will need the following items:

- A lodestone
- A pouch
- Hair from the head of your beloved
- Scraping from the sole of the shoe of your beloved
- A piece of paper

Write the name of your beloved on the piece of paper and put all of the items listed above into the pouch. Hold the pouch close to your heart and express your intentions clearly. This is not the time to evoke wishful thinking. Be clear about what you want them to feel and visualize your energy transferring to the bag in that moment. After this visual exercise, breathe on the bag and then keep it close to you at all times. The spell will be activated.

Spell Four: Stay on Their Mind

Purpose: To keep your beloved thinking about you constantly

They say that absence makes the heart grow fonder but sometimes what you need to keep that love going is for you to be on their mind all day. You can achieve this with a very simple home spell. You need:

- Crushed lodestone (1 tbsp)
- Crushed thyme (1 tbsp)
- A scoop of your bathwater

Mix all of these ingredients together in a bowl and find a way to pour it at the entryway of the home of your beloved. Obviously, if you share a home together, that is ideal. If not, you will have to think of an excuse to spill this at their door. Bear in mind at all times the intention that you have for this spell. You do not need to speak it into existence, but your intentions matter.

Spell Five: Follow Me Boy Oil

Purpose: To attract luck, love, wealth, and to make you stand out

- Angelica root
- Catnip herb
- Coriander seed
- Damiana herb

- Fennel seed
- Grapeseed oil (use almond oil for a sweetening effect)

Mix all of these herbs together and pour into the oil. Allow it to sit in a warm place for a few days. Shake every now and then during that time and you are good to go.

SPELLS FOR MONEY AND LUCK

A s with every other spell I have described, this type of magic will not create something out of nothing. Instead, it works as a magnet for the thing that you desire. In this case, money. When you are setting your expectations, it is important to be realistic about it so that it aligns with your intentions. If you are hoping that somehow money will fall from the sky or that a tree in your garden will suddenly start sprouting dollar leaves, you will be disappointed. However, a more realistic expectation would be the hope that your business will begin booming or that you will find favor with financially influential people who would be happy to share their wealth with you. In this chapter, I am going to talk about how you can use the elements in our environment to make this happen.

Using the Elements to Attract Money

Attracting money and creating a sustainable source of income is a desire that we all have and is not a wish to be ashamed of. As we all know, wealth does not always go to the most hardworking among us. It goes to those who have the greatest opportunities and know what to do with those opportunities. Hoodoo spells work with this kind of logic. You are not tipping the balance of power by being greedy. Instead, you are bending the elements that guide and control wealth and manipulating them to do your bidding. You receive wealth by ensuring that the right conditions are aligned to deliver the results that you want.

My grandmother used to say that wealth is attained when you are able to fulfill the criteria for it. Sometimes, that criteria could be about attracting favor, being in the presence of the right person at the right time or generally attracting people who are able to fulfill your financial needs. It is hard to describe how it works except to say that, as my grandmother says, money spells help you create the conditions for wealth. When you are working on a money spell, try not to focus on the "hows." Instead, reflect on the purpose that drives you and use that as an anchor to create the spell.

There are a lot of untruths and misconceptions surrounding the creation of wealth through Hoodoo spells, and while I cannot list all of these or address them right now, I will tell you that there is no spell that can make you rich overnight. There are some spells that increase your chances in games of luck, for instance, if you gamble or play the lotto. But even then, I would discourage you from having grand visions of living in luxury. On the flip side, it is likely that your luck will change because you will suddenly find open doors that had been closed to you in the past, and if you are running a business, you might even have an inflow of clients and customers.

Changing Your Luck

If we consider the concept of luck from a clinical perspective, it is difficult to understand why certain people appear to have more of it than others. There have been many studies conducted to determine why this is so. One particular study showed that people who seem lucky tend to be more outgoing and extroverted. They tend to have a more cheerful disposition when compared to people who are considered "unlucky." If you keep this in mind and think about how Hoodoo works, you will find similarities in the patterns of all the spells, in that they are meant to create the right conditions to bring about the desired results, and that a cheerful disposition is a component in each one.

Hoodoo magic is not about snapping your fingers or waving a magical wand and having everything click into position for you. It is more about aligning the elements in your favor, if you find that you are one of those people who has struggled with bad luck for a long time. This spell is going to condition your mind as well as the universal elements surrounding your situation to bring about the results you want. I have said many times that one of the most powerful ingredients in a spell is your intention, and it is your intention that will help your spell manifest.

When you activate a luck spell in your life, you are conditioning yourself emotionally, mentally and physically to be more aware of the opportunities that are available to you in your environment. But it goes a step further. It attracts those opportunities to you so that you have more chances to attain the life you want. When you have more chances, there is greater possibility that the results you want will manifest. So when you have all of this in mind as you proceed to the next set of spells, you are in a better position to visualize what you want to become a reality.

5 MONEY SPELLS TO ATTRACT MONEY

Spell One: Luck Draw Mojo

Purpose: Increasing luck in the area of money attraction and bringing good fortune

The main ingredient for this spell can be found at a blacksmith's. If you don't have a blacksmith close to you, magnetic sand, which can be purchased in most Hoodoo stores, is an excellent substitute. You will need:

- A red flannel pouch
- Anvil dust (magnetic sand)
- Garlic (clove)
- Lodestone
- Sugar
- Whiskey

Put the garlic clove and lodestone in the red flannel pouch. Sprinkle the anvil dust (or magnetic sand) and the sugar on the pouch. Sew the flannel shut. As you do this, speak your intentions to the bag. When you are finished, soak the bag in whiskey and you are good to go.

Spell Two: Quick Cash Fire

Purpose: To attract urgent money for those days when you are having an emergency that requires money to solve it

This is one of those spells that is so simple, you might question its effectiveness, but I can promise you that if you are able to put this together, the outcome is quick. Don't expect to become a billionaire overnight, though. This is more about getting urgent cash fast. In addition to your intent, gather these items:

- Bay leaf
- Cinnamon (powdered)
- Nutmeg (powdered)

Mix a generous quantity of these ingredients together. Light a candle to center your focus if you are having problems gathering your thoughts. You need to have a singular intent to which this spell will be directed. If, for instance, you need this money for your rent, focus on the exact amount you need and call for it. Next, burn the mixture. You should get an immediate mix of flavors and scents. Fan the smoke towards you and try to absorb as much of it as possible. It's important that your hands and face absorb the smoke. When you are through, discard the remnants and remain expectant.

~

Spell Three: The Moneyball

Purpose: To attract cash and fulfill the atmospheric conditions for sustainable prosperity

The previous spell was for petty or fast cash. This one helps to grow your overall wealth. Again, I have to caution you that this is not going to happen overnight. But if you maintain your attitude and intention for the spell, you will find it manifesting in your life sooner than later. To get the money ball spell running, you will need the following ingredients:

- Dry basil
- Green cotton thread
- High John root
- Name paper

Begin the spell by wrapping the basil leaves around the high john root. On the name paper write your name and expectation and wrap the paper around the leaves. Use the green thread to tie this paper. To increase your money attraction, you can coat the thread with fast cash oil if you have it. Wrap the thread around the package nine times and leave some extra thread hanging so you can tie it somewhere and dangle it. Choose somewhere private to hang this and every day afterward, tap it to swing in a circle and recite Psalm 23 as it swings. To keep the spell active, rub it every week or so with fast cash oil or any other money oil.

. . .

Spell Four: Debt Dissolved

Purpose: To get rid of debt or create financial report problems that work in your favor by dissolving your debt

If you owe someone money or you find yourself in a predicament where money is being demanded of you, you can take care of the problem by carrying out this spell. All you need is:

- Two medium-sized onions (preferably red onions)
- Piece of paper with your name on it

Write your name on the paper nine times and then turn it over. Write the amount that you owe but do it backwards. Write this number nine times. Now fold the paper and burn it to ash. Cut the two onions in half and rub the ashes from the burnt paper on the exposed side of each of these onions. Place the onion with the ash coated on it in each of the four corners of your home. Remember to keep your intention in mind as you do this. The problem will be solved.

Spell Five: Lucky Cologne

Purpose: This is used to attract luck and can also be used as spray perfume for candles, mojos and other spells that involve attracting luck

This spell is used as a juice booster for the other spells that you create. You can also put it on you when you go out if you need to attract some luck to whatever activity you are engaging in. It doesn't matter if it is a love spell or a money spell that you want to boost. This particular cologne will increase the chances of that spell becoming effective because of its luck attraction. You just need:

- Orange peels
- Rum
- 9 nutmegs

Put the orange peels into a bottle of quality rum, but do not mix them. Recite the following chant as you shake it: *"This is a message to all my kin, below and above, I want you to make me very lucky... in wealth and in love."* Repeat this chant until you experience a release in your spirit and then place the bottle in the sun for nine days. At the start of each day, shake the bottle and repeat the chant. On the ninth day, your lucky cologne is ready to use.

11

SPELLS FOR SUCCESS

This is another one of those spells that is going to work actively with the image you paint in your mind. The reason for this is simple; success means different things to different people. For some people, having an abundance of wealth is success. For others, passing exams, getting married or convincing someone to give them a business contract is how they define success. Whatever that definition is to you, it is important to hold that image in your mind. You cannot think of success in a broad and general sense because when your desires begin to manifest based on a spell, it will be difficult to identify what is manifesting as a result of that spell. This is why it's important that you have a clearly defined image in mind before creating a success spell. In this chapter, I want to explore the concept of success and help you figure out ways to fine-tune what you want your spell to do for you. It will have a lot to do with attracting luck, wealth and generally maintaining balance in your environment. When you have balance and harmony in your environment, it is easier for things to align themselves with your will.

Using Hoodoo to Invite Positive Change

In order to grow in life, change is necessary. If you look at things from this perspective, you will agree with me that change is one of the prerequisites for growth, and when you have upward growth, you will most likely experience success. We could even say that change is the precursor to success. Keeping this in mind, one of the first things you should train yourself to think about is the kind of changes that you believe will bring about the success you want to see in your life.

For example, your goal could be to simply become successful at losing that extra 10 pounds you gained in the last year or so. For that to happen, you cannot continue to sit on the couch, eat the same thing over and over and lead a sedentary lifestyle, and still expect that transformation to occur. Success in that regard will mean a change in lifestyle and habits. This will now draw your focus towards your mindset. A proper change in your attitude towards health can be the thing that will trigger your successful weight loss journey. This is just one of the ways you can condition your mind to initiate the changes that will bring about the success you want.

It doesn't matter whether you are studying for an exam or applying for a job or even planning to propose to someone. The transformation process required of the mind is pretty much the same. You need to think of the right condition that will bring about the manifestation of the success you desire. The first step you need to take is to identify what exactly you consider success. The more specific you are about the objective, the higher the chances you have for that spell to work. When you have clearly defined this outcome, the next step is to think of the mental state of mind that you have to be in to bring about this change.

When you focus on other people, you lose sight of the power that you have inside yourself and when you fail to acknowledge this power, how can you hope to power up your spell? Yes, you can draw on insight and strength from your ancestors, but it is your link to them that will fire up the power that they lend to you. This means all roads eventually lead back to you. For this reason, I want you to start thinking of that thing you can do on the inside, as well as the mindset you can develop to create that additional ginger that will drive you towards your success objective. When you have this sorted out, you are on track to creating a powerful success spell.

The Key Ingredients for Manifesting Success in Different Areas

As I explained in the previous segment, manifesting success in any area is linked to your ability to aptly and accurately define what that success means to you. Your imagination is going to be one of the most crucial ingredients, which is why it is advisable that moments before you create your spell, you light a candle and meditate to give yourself clarity on the subject. After you have obtained clarity, write out what you see in a journal or on sheet of paper. Read over and over again what you have written down until it becomes a solid image in your mind. This image should be so strong that it almost feels as if you could reach out and touch it. This is how vivid it should be before you step into the place where you create the spell. Hold that image in your mind when you cast the spell.

There are also external conditions that must be fulfilled for a success spell to manifest. Each spell has its own unique identity, which means that it also has individual terms for the fulfillment of the spell's contract. For example, if you are dealing with finances, you need to invoke the aid of elements such as green colors, plant spirits associated with money, and stones that are known to attract money. For a success spell that involves coercion, your willpower is going to be a required ingredient or condition that has to be met. If your willpower is not strong enough, it will be impossible to coerce the other person to do your bidding.

I remember creating a "cheat no more" love potion mix for a client. Her husband was a chronic womanizer who was known in the neighborhood for his infidelity, and this embarrassed her to no end. She wanted to put an end to this behavior. However, she had a very timid and docile personality, which made it difficult for her to command him to stop this action even in absentia. So I had to work on her intonation, mindset and expectation in order for the spell to become fully activated. The second she got it right, the husband stopped his philandering ways. Understand what the conditions of the spell are and endeavor to fulfill all of them. Remember, this goes beyond acquiring ingredients.

5 SUCCESS SPELLS YOU CAN TRY TODAY

Spell One: Save Me From Poverty

Purpose: To quickly draw you from the brink of poverty by ensuring that quick cash, usually $5,000 and below, locates you immediately

There are times when you find you are completely broke, no matter how well you saved your money. Rather than panic about the situation, draw on the elements in your environment for financial sustenance. Success in this regard is about having enough to take care of your basic needs, so that is exactly what the spell is for. To complete it, you would need the following items:

- 1 green 7-day candle
- Dried and ground ginger
- Black tea leaves
- Peppermint essential oil

Poke three holes in a straight line on the top of the candle. Pour four drops of the peppermint oil into one hole. Mix the ginger and black tea together and put a pinch of this mixture into the remaining two holes on the candle. Next, take a piece of paper and write on it the exact amount of money you need. Remember, it cannot exceed $5,000. Turn the paper and sign your name on it three times. Then burn the paper as you say these words: "Holy ones, help me. Bring me a gift and grant me what I need." Recite these words 12 times over the candle, after which you can put it out. For the next seven days, you must repeat the cycle of writing the amount of money you need on the paper with your signature and burning it while you recite the words. Expect to receive the gifts in the following days.

Spell Two: Golden Luck Bath Oil

Purpose: To activate good fortunes

This is more of a blending type of spell than it is an invocation. In other words, you are merging elements together to create a desired magical condition. So you do not need special incantations or to perform it at specific times. If you have all the ingredients, mix them together and bless it with your intentions and you are good to go. The ingredients needed for this are:

- Citroen chips
- Gold mica powder
- Lavender oil
- Orange oil
- Olive oil

Mix all of these elements together and pour the mixture into a transparent glass bottle and you have your golden luck oil. Every time you take a bath, put a few drops in to attract the kind of success you desire, whether it is in business partnerships, new relationships or money-related issues. It works for me every time.

Spell Three: Golden Prosper Bath

Purpose: To bring and attract wealth and money into your home, business and person

In addition to the bath oil I just described, you can create a bath spell that activates wealth in your center, thus attracting success to you at every turn. The ingredients are very basic but might need to be purchased at a local Hoodoo store. You need:

- Goldenseal root (One or two roots)
- Marigold petals (two large handfuls)
- Sassafras leaves (two large handfuls)
- Water (holy water if you can find it)

Pour all the herbs together into a gallon of water and boil the water. Once it boils, pour it into a strainer to separate the herbs from the water. Recite Psalm 4 as you stir the water clockwise. When you have finished, the spell is ready. Bury the herbs somewhere in the garden afterwards. You can use the water with your bath for purification purposes as outlined in the chapter about purification baths or you can use it to clean your home as described in the cleansing ritual. If you are using it for your place of business, the best practice is to put it into a spray bottle and spritz it all over your work space. Make sure to spray it on fabrics like curtains, chairs and so on.

Spell Four: Big Man Cologne

Purpose: To attract successful relationships in business, friendship and romantic life. Also, to project an aura of power and success

This one is specifically for guys. As a man, it is important that you present your A game at all times. However, this is not always easy. This spell will give you a leg up and set the tone for the life that you are hoping to live. You will need:

- Bay leaves
- Dixie John root
- Juniper berries
- Lemon grass
- Lemon peel
- Your favorite cologne

Pour all these herbs into a bottle containing your favorite cologne. Allow them to soak there for at least 12 days. Store this mixture in a dark place during these 12 days to allow it to absorb the essence of the herbs. At the end of the 12th day, shake it vigorously to stir up everything and then strain it into another container. Bury the herbs and keep the cologne. Use this on your person when you want to attract success. Rub it on your pillow and beddings to attract romance. Spritz a little on your wallet and hands for business success.

Spell Five: Prosper Me Wash

Purpose: To open up new paths and usher in success

Cleanse your immediate environment, whether it's your home or business, and create a new pathway for success with this simple but potent spell. All you need are four ingredients:

- Lemon grass
- Magnolia petals
- Peppermint leaves
- Water

Mix two handfuls of each herb into 3 quarts of water. Boil the water. Meditate and pray on the scripture Psalm 23 while the mixture is boiling. When it is ready, pour it into a strainer and discard the herbs under running water. This symbolizes old things going away. Use the water from the mixture to wash the floors, walls, windows and door frames of either your home or business or the place to which you want to attract success. Do this once a week for five weeks. The best time to do it is on a Friday at dawn.

12

SPELLS FOR PROTECTION

"...You will not fear the terror of the night
Nor the arrow that flies by day...
For He will command his angels concerning you
To guard you in all your ways..."
Psalm 91

S afety is a priority for everyone, regardless of where you live. Sometimes the danger that we face is a physical one and could threaten our lives. Other times, the danger is spiritual, which can also threaten our lives but starts its damage by crippling us from the inside. A protection spell in Hoodoo practice serves to keep you physically, mentally and spiritually protected and helps to keep out negative energy and ensure that the space you are in is constantly feeding you with the kind of energy that preserves, calms and uplifts you. In this chapter, we will delve into the less common practice of spiritual preservation.

Because of our attachment to logical thinking and reasoning, not many of us understand the pull from the other side. Some of us are spiritually alert and can sense certain auras or spirits around us. But for the most part, people tend to be blissfully unaware of the threats posed by these entities. The impacts they could have on the quality of your life can be felt in physical ways, and this is why it is important to protect yourself at all times. When you practice Hoodoo, you acknowledge the presence of these entities and spirits, and with each step of your journey, the spirit becomes more aware of you. Sometimes, their awareness of your presence could be dangerous for you. I will explain all of this in more detail as we continue.

Protection from Physical and Spiritual Attacks

The practice of Hoodoo is a spiritual one. You are embarking on a journey every single day that connects you with your inner goddess/god and this makes you aware of the entities in your environment. I would love to tell you that the journey is always beautiful and peaceful and full of gentle awakening. However, just as there are good spirits with good intentions, there are also bad spirits with bad intentions. There are malevolent entities whose mission is simply to ruin lives. I have personally had tough spiritual cases that involved individuals who were touched by these evil spirits, even though they had no idea that such spirits existed. They had a lot of negative manifestations in their lives and it felt as if they were simply going from one problem to another. Sadly, these manifestations of evil are not limited to individual experiences.

Inanimate objects can also be touched by negative influences. You have probably watched horror movies where people move into a home where there is an entity that threatens their lives. While entertaining as a movie, the truth is that this happens in real life. There are homes that are haunted by the spirits of people who inhabited them. There are also situations in which people are living under a curse. A curse is not simply negative words spoken against you. It entails the binding of evil forces to a person, so it feels as if that person is always under a negative cloud, no matter where they go. These curses can be incurred both knowingly and unknowingly. You may accidentally come in contact with objects that are cursed and for that singular act you are penalized. You may also have dealings with people who are cursed and through your relationship with them you attract their curse into your own life.

I could go on and on, listing the physical and spiritual dangers that are ever present in our environment, but my objective is not to scare you or cause you anxiety but to prepare you for this journey that you are about to undertake. Being a Hoodoo practitioner means that you acknowledge these things that I have talked about, but rather than feel helpless, you are empowered to banish, or at least restrict their influence over your life and over the lives of the people you love. In this chapter, you will learn how to remove/nullify common curses, sanctify personal spaces and keep negative energy and entities out of your life. The spells, as with all the other spells in this book, are uncomplicated but very effective.

Protecting Inanimate Objects

Transference of energy from a person to an object or from a spirit to an object is a real thing. This is why our ancestors developed the craft of blessing certain objects to help amplify the spells we are creating and also to unify your intents. A protection spell over an inanimate object does not necessarily mean that you are binding powers to that object. What you are doing is transferring energy and intent to that object and using it as a beacon to attract what you want. For example, you could cast a protection spell over your home to attract benevolent spirits, positive energy and create an active force field to keep out anything that wants to cause you harm. This is very important for any Hoodoo practitioner because as you begin your journey, you will find that you are becoming more spiritually enlightened with each passing day and are therefore more open spiritually, which means you will attract both good and bad entities.

It is important that the place where you practice your craft the most, which is probably your home, is fully cloaked and protected, especially in the early stages. You do this so that these malevolent entities do not take advantage of your spiritual youthfulness and invade your space. A protection spell cloaks you from the eyes of evil and wicked men. It also ensures that spirits that do not have your best interests at heart are unable to enter into your space. A protection spell over your home casts out negative energy and creates an atmosphere that enables and empowers your spells. Your home is your first line of defense. It is also your altar and your spiritual launch pad. You would do well to ensure that you are strongest in this place at all times. The spells you create to carry around with you will be an extension of the force you are able to create in your home.

There are purification baths you can carry out to cleanse and protect you physically and spiritually. Then there are objects to which you can transfer spiritual energy and carry around with you when you are mobile. These objects often imbibe your intentions and your reach to ancestral powers, who are very helpful when it comes to building powerful protection spells. As you grow in the craft, you will be able to create runes, marks and spells that alert you the moment you come in contact with a vile entity. The reaction to this warning can be so intense that you experience pain and nausea, or even have a seizure. Creating these powerful spells is not something for beginners. It is something you will learn as you grow. For now, here are some steps you can take to keep you safe as you continue to practice your craft.

5 SIMPLE BUT POWERFUL PROTECTION SPELLS

Spell One: Black Salt Powder

Purpose: for protecting stationary or inanimate objects like your home, jewelry or even the area where you cast your spell. You can also use it as a protection spell for a person

Protection spells commonly use circles. In Hoodoo magic, drawing circles is a form of basic ritualistic practice. You use certain elements to create circles around what you are blessing, cursing, protecting or empowering with your spell. It is no different in this situation. The black salt that you create should be used in a circle around the person object or space that you want to protect. Here is what you need:

- Black pepper
- Charcoal
- Salt
- Wood ash

Put all ingredients together in a mortar and grind them using the same movement as the clock hand. Ensure that everything mixes smoothly and evenly. Empty the contents into a bowl and bless it with a prayer from Psalm 91. Use the salt powder to make circles around anything or any person you want to protect.

Spell Two: Be Gone Fire

Purpose: To remove specific things that you no longer want in your life

Before you initiate this spell, take a moment to sit down and think about something that has been bothering you lately. Concentrate on this singular thing. Form the words that accurately describe this thing. When you are certain that you have it in your mind, you can begin. You will need these items:

- Bay leaves
- Lemon grass
- Peanut shells
- White onion skin

Make a fire in an outside space. When you have a nice fire going, write on a bay leaf exactly what you wish to banish from your life. It could be the one thing you have been concentrating on or it could be a list of things. If it is a list of things, use one bay leaf for each thing. Pour the bay leaves and all the other ingredients into a bowl. Stir it counterclockwise and repeat these words nine times: "That which I have written, send away forever." When you are finished, burn the mixture in the fire. Do not inhale the smoke. When everything has burned down, let it cool and find somewhere far away to bury the ashes.

Spell Three: Hard Day Cleanse

Purpose: To get rid of negative energy and exhaustion

Energy plays a role in enhancing the atmosphere and making it conducive for your spells to thrive. If you find yourself having a rough day, this spell will wash off the remnants of these negative emotions and set you on a path to healing and restoration. You will need the following:

- Eucalyptus leaves
- Lemon peels
- Peppermint leaves
- Rosemary
- White cheese cloth

All the ingredients should be fresh. Tie them up in the white cheese cloth. Pour a hot bath and steep this cloth with the herbs in the hot water, stirring it counterclockwise. Inhale the steam that comes from this activity and keep at it until the water becomes cool enough for you to get in. Remove the herbs from the cloth and set them aside for disposal later. Immerse yourself completely in the water for a few seconds. As you emerge, visualize a light filling you up on the inside and washing over you on the outside. Get out of the bath and air dry yourself. Throw the remnants of the spell far away from your home.

Spell Four: Protection from Evil

Purpose: To provide active protection against spiritual or physical harm

Regardless of whether or not you practice Hoodoo, there are people you will meet in this life who will immediately set your teeth on edge. All the alarms in your body go off but you don't know why you feel this way about them. This is usually an indication that that person could be dangerous, so this spell is designed to protect you from these kinds of people. You can also activate it to protect someone you care about from these very same people. It is potent but is also something you can do as a beginner. You will need the following items:

- Blue 7-day candle
- Camphor essential oil
- Cloves
- Dried onions
- Name paper

Grind the cloves and dried onions together. Mix them up thoroughly and set aside. Next, poke three holes on the top of the candle. In the first hole, pour four drops of camphor essential oil. In the other two holes, put a pinch of the dried herbs. Next, write out the name of the person you want the spell to protect and place the paper underneath the candle. Pick a scripture of protection that you like. My personal favorite is always going to be Psalm 91. Recite this scripture as you gaze into the light of the candle. The purpose of this is to center your thoughts and your intent. Draw on the energy that you receive and direct it towards the person. You will experience a sense of calm wash over you at the end of the recital. Put out the candle and repeat this process every day for the next seven days.

Spell Five: Reputation Saver

Purpose: to silence the voices of people who may have something evil and negative to say about you and to preserve your reputation

In this day and age, where a single tweet can undermine years of hard work, it is important to ensure that your reputation is able to stand the test of time. This protection spell helps to keep your name off of the lips of people who might say something negative about you. It helps silence gossip and rumor mongers. To initiate you spell, you need:

- Dirt from crossroads
- Paper with your name on it
- Reversing oil/Shut up oil/Stop gossip oil
- Silver dime
- String to tie the spell
- Sunflower seeds

Write your name in bold on a piece of paper with jagged edges. Pour nine drops of your preferred oil on the paper. Put the silver dime, dirt from the crossroads and sunflower seeds on the paper. Fold it up neatly and tie the string around it to secure it. Hold it close to your lips and repeat these words nine times: *"I bind all that speak evil of me."* The spell is cast. You can place it on your person by putting it in a bag or in your pocket and ensure that is with you at all times.

13

SPELLS FOR JUSTICE

Life, they say, is not fair. You cannot truly understand this statement until you find yourself in a position where you feel as if you have been deprived of justice. And while it is benevolent to sit by and wait for karma to work, sometimes you feel like you have to do something yourself, and the only way to create a balance, or at least tip the scale of justice in your favor, is to intervene spiritually. This is where spells of justice come in. This does not automatically mean that everything is going to be okay. Granted, revenge feels good when your perceived enemy is being made to suffer for the things they have put you through. However, it doesn't always bring about the satisfaction that you seek. With this in mind, it is important to understand the elements at play when you decide to cast a justice spell.

Invoking Ancestral Spirits for Aid

When you practice Hoodoo, one of the things you will quickly come to learn is the fact that we do not actively believe in karma. As you continue to grow in the craft, perhaps you will also come to see things from my point of view. Even so, because of our Christian roots, many of us are guided by strong moral and ethical beliefs. When you decide to cast a spell of justice, you are usually filled with righteous indignation and there is no one who will understand this pain better than ancestors who share your blood and come from the same root as you. Each and every one of us has suffered some form of injustice at some point in our lives, and it is possible that we will not live long enough to get the justice that we deserve.

When you call upon the spirits of the ancestors for spells like these, they are most willing to aid you. Their assistance is relied on heavily for these types of spells because it helps account for that karmic element. In Hoodoo practice, this isn't talked about in general circles, but this is what our ancestors do when they help us. If they offer their assistance with the spell you are creating, they also take up the burden that comes from dabbling in these sensitive matters. In other words, you do the magic that they help you to activate, but they deal with the consequences. So luckily, there really isn't much for you to lose. However, you must ensure that in rendering the spell, you pay proper homage to them by offering sacrifices worthy of their involvement. Every spell, as I have said continually throughout this book, has a condition to be fulfilled. With a justice spell, most of what you need to do is ensure that your ancestors are appeased. They will handle the rest.

Karma, Vengeance and Justice

As I told you earlier, karma is not a concept that we think about in Hoodoo practice. As long as you fulfill the conditions of the spell and ensure that it is rooted and balanced, you are fine. In a case where emotions might be running high, the spell might be unstable, so involving the help of your ancestors can help mitigate the consequences of casting an unstable spell. Again, this really has nothing to do with karma. It is more about retaining balance between good and bad, and ensuring that your intentions are aligned with the properties of the spell that you create.

Vengeance is a powerful emotion, especially when it is motivated by pain. The stronger the pain, the higher the rage and thirst for revenge and this has a way of clouding your judgment. In the introductory chapters of this book, I talked about how important it is to have clarity of mind and centered focus in the delivery and rendering of the spell that you want. Distorting it with emotions can create an imbalance that will have an adverse effect. Much like in cooking, you have to make sure that the salt balances out the other flavors in the soup. If it overpowers the other flavors, the result will not be appealing. This does not mean that karma is serving you, it is simply a consequence of an action or inaction. Keeping this in mind, let us look at 5 simple spells that can help to bring you justice or tip the scales of the law in your favor.

GETTING JUSTICE WITH 5 UNIQUE SPELLS

Spell One: Make it Stop

Purpose: To temporarily hold off people from taking legal action until you are ready to deal with the situation

This is particularly helpful if you find yourself in the middle of a court case for which you are totally unprepared. You know that it can be a time-consuming process, not to mention the amount of money that will be required for legal fees and to sway justice in your favor. So until you are ready to deal with it, you can set the spell in motion. The spell is quick, easy and doesn't require too much. You need:

- A piece of paper
- A transparent jar

Write on a sheet of paper everything you are going through with the court case. Focus particularly on the charges that have been made against you and what your worries are about the case. Insert this paper into a jar of water and put it in the freezer. The spell is done. As long as that water stays frozen, the case or pending legalities will be frozen. However, bear in mind that this is only temporary. It does not stop the problem, it simply puts it on hold.

Spell Two: Hot Sauce Revenge

Purpose: To cause the people who hurt you to physically suffer

Revenge, they say, is a dish best served cold. But sometimes, all you need is a little hot sauce and that revenge will have a rewarding taste in your mouth. The star player in a revenge spell is hot sauce. I would advise that you find the hottest sauce available over the counter if you really want to inflict revenge on this person. Don't worry. The person on the receiving end of this spell will not die or experience anything inhumane, but they will suffer. You should get:

- Hot sauce
- A doll, figurine or candle

Begin by baptizing the candle, doll, figurine or whatever you are using as a physical representation of the person on whom you want to cast a spell. If you do not know the name of the person (often the case when you have been slighted or hurt anonymously), you can simply tag the doll: "whoever did xyz to you." "Xyz" obviously represents the action or hurt that was carried out against you. When you have consecrated the doll in their name, pour hot sauce all over it. Ensure that it is completely covered and leave it out in the sun. As the hot sauce dries on the figurine or candle, the person for whom the spell is intended will begin to experience inexplicable heat and will develop welt marks on their bodies.

Spell Three: Dry Up Their Love

Purpose: To completely break up a relationship without drama or negative consequences

We have all been in the situation where our beloved or someone we care about is having an entanglement with an ex. This spell is designed to put an end to that by simply drying out whatever affection they have for each other and causing them to drift apart. You need:

- Burned matches
- Jar
- Name paper
- Pins
- Salt
- Sand
- Red rosebud

Put a handful of burned matches into an equal part mixture of salt and sand. Write down the name of your beloved on one paper and their object of affection on another. Fold this name paper into the rosebud. Use the pins to pierce this rosebud with the name papers inside. This will quickly end their sexual connection. Pour the sand, salt and burned matches mixture into a jar. Put the rose with the pin piercings into this jar. Seal it and bury it in a graveyard. Put your mind at ease and you will witness the slow, gradual but definite decay of that relationship.

Spell Four: Storm Head Work

Purpose: To torment and torture your enemy

There is no peace for the wicked, and if you really want to be your own angel of vengeance, you can drop this spell to ensure that your enemies have no peace. Just remember to center your energy and emotions before activating this spell. Here is what you will need:

- A black string
- Black marker
- Coconut

First baptize the coconut in the name of your enemy by submerging it in water and chanting these words: "I baptize you (say your enemy's name). This coconut is now your head. Whatever happens to this coconut will happen to you." Repeat this three times and then proceed to activate the spell. With the black marker, write out what you want to happen to this person on the coconut. For example, you could say, "experience incurable headaches" or "move far away" or "lose your wallet." Whatever your petition is, write it on the coconut. This spell is best performed on the eve of a storm, so that as soon as you are finished writing your petition, you hang it on a tree outside. If the coconut is gone after the storm has passed, you can take it as a sign that the spirits have answered your petition. If it's still hanging there, break it down and break it with a hammer. Your intentions will still manifest in the life of your enemy.

Spell Five: Protection from Harm Bottle

Purpose: To prevent against arrest, abuse and injustice

If you find yourself in a situation where any of these three things is bound to happen; an arrest, physical abuse or injustice, a spell like this can activate protection over you that will stop this from happening. This spell is one of the earlier spells my grandmother taught me and its power is still relevant in today's atmosphere. The ingredients are:

- Black feathers
- Hard liquor
- Name paper
- Oregano
- Salt

Write down the name of the person you want to protect. Place it inside the bottle of liquor. Put the oregano, black feathers and salt in the same bottle, then seal the bottle. If it makes you feel more comfortable, you can back up this process by reciting a protection prayer from your favorite verse in the Bible. When you have finished doing that, shake it 11 times and store it outside your back door whenever you sense problems associated with arrest, abuse or injustice. When you are through with it, you can store it in a dry place until you need it again.

CONCLUSION

I have trained many people in the sacred craft of Hoodoo practice, and writing this book gives me the same pleasure I derive from seeing my students thrive. I hope that using this book you are able to get clarity on some of the problems you are experiencing and will become empowered by the spells I have shared. More than this, it is my desire that you become an active part of our small and unique community of Hoodoo practitioners. Even as this book comes to an end, I want to encourage you to keep searching, keep growing and keep learning. There is so much information out there and the more you connect yourself with it, the more our ancestors will reward you.

Being a Hoodoo practitioner is more than just casting spells and changing your destiny. It is about aligning yourself with your spiritual purpose and I am thankful and honored to be a part of your process. As you close this book, meditate on some of the lessons that you have learned here. Especially the ones that deeply resonated with you.

From time to time, re-read the book to find clarity on things that may have not offered enlightenment the first time you read about them. If you have friends who are equally curious, share with them the knowledge that you have gained. I believe that our world becomes a better place when knowledge is shared. Unlike the olden days, when Hoodoo was relegated to dark and mysterious corners of the world, today we are openly practicing our craft and we are proud of it.

I want you to share in this pride. If this is your calling, pursue it diligently. You will be amazed by the results and blessings that will come your way as a result. Since the day I took up the mantle of my grandmother, I have never regretted a moment of it. I have been on a rollercoaster of emotions, from joy to anguish to sorrow when I hear some of the things that my clients are going through. But the emotion that stands out above all others is pride. I take pride in seeing people take their place in their community because of the opportunities that have become available to them... opportunities that without Hoodoo magic might not have presented themselves. You are now presented with a unique opportunity. Grab it with both hands and use it to change your world. I hope that one day our paths will cross, and I will hear your story too. Until then, stay blessed.

CPSIA information can be obtained
at www.ICGtesting.com
Printed in the USA
LVHW080755040821
694505LV00002B/40